Reef and Beach
Life of New Zealand

An Introduction by

Michael Miller and Gary Batt

Collins
Auckland and London

FIRST PUBLISHED 1973
WILLIAM COLLINS (NEW ZEALAND) LTD.,
P.O. BOX NO. 1, AUCKLAND

Acknowledgements

We wish to thank two people for their help: Barbara, Gary's wife, for typing the manuscript and Mr W. E. Forde, the Editor of Collins in New Zealand, who encouraged us to write this book, gently prodding us when we slacked and giving assistance when we encountered difficulties.

© Michael Miller and Gary Batt 1973

Printed in Hong Kong by
Dai Nippon Printing Co., (H.K.) Ltd.

Contents

Illustrations

Preface

Few people are very familiar with the plants and animals of the seashore. This may seem surprising since the seashore is the most visited part of the New Zealand natural environment. Memories of a trip to the seaside are usually the tang of the sea, the invigorating breezes, the sun glinting on the sea and wet sand, and the good sport; if the natural inhabitants are recalled at all it is the taste of a meal of pipis, rock oysters or sea eggs. It seems a pity that an appreciation and understanding of seashore life is restricted to some senior school pupils (unfortunately their biology lessons are soon forgotten), members of certain natural history societies and a few professional biologists. The creatures themselves may be to blame for their not being widely known; their strange appearance, small size and retiring habits may discourage anything less than the most persistent interest. It may be, however, that the lack of a suitable introduction is the reason for their obscurity: believing this more likely, we have prepared this book.

We have made a great effort to present the subject in simple language; you will find the text devoid of all those names and terms forming the language of biology which, for the uninitiated, are so difficult to pronounce and render reading jerky and disconcerting. The only concession which we have not made is to discard the scientific names of the plants and animals: many of these organisms have no common or popular names and it certainly would be presumptuous of us to make them up here; also, some common names vary from place to place, and often a name may be applied to different species – scientific names are more reliable and international. It is only the lack of confidence and practice which make one hesitate or stumble when pronouncing a Latin or Latinized name for the first time; few people have difficulty with *Rhinoceros, Hippopotamus* and *Chrysanthemum*, names which are as awkward to say as any in this book.

11

Reef and Beach Life of New Zealand

Your attention is drawn to certain important features of shore life neglected in our simplified account. Patterns of life differ in detail from one point to another on the same piece of shore, even where the habitat is perfectly uniform. These small differences result from the activities of past generations of shore organisms, the growth or behaviour of individuals or because of some chance happening. Over wider distances some species are replaced by others – this is due to differences in their geographical ranges (principally governed by water temperatures). We hope our professional colleagues who read our book will understand and forgive us for ignoring these and other points which complicate the subject.

Throughout our book we write of zones of organisms, but these are only really obvious and precise in sessile types. Because of their wanderings or wide spacing, the zones of mobile animals are only recognizable after careful observation. You must remember too that low tide on the shore is a time of rest: to see some of the larger animals out making a living you need to sit, equipped with aqualung and mask, on the shore when it is covered by the sea or to go out at low tide on a humid night. Many of the shore animals are small and shy and can only be observed properly when placed in a dish or small aquarium and watched through a microscope of low magnification (10–40x): for this reason most of the species we have described can be seen easily with the naked eye. The colour of most of the species mentioned is given, but we do remind you that no two individuals of the same species are identical; often you will find specimens which do not fit our descriptions exactly.

Enjoy the seashore but treat it kindly for it is most precious. The seashore offers us all, present and future generations, an easy opportunity to see and learn something of the wonderfully rich life of the sea. When you go to the shore disturb the plants and animals as little as possible. If you move or turn over a stone or rock, remember to return it to its original position right side up: those organisms fixed permanently to the surface will die if you do not for they cannot crawl away to their proper site. Do not take home any organism unless you really need it for serious study.

12

Shore, Tides and Waves

The shore is where sea and land meet. It cannot, however, be properly described quite so simply, for on our coasts, as in other parts of the world, the sea advances and retreats across the shore every day. This movement of the sea across the shore is called the tide. Since the edge of the sea is constantly on the move, we might then say that the shore is that strip of land which lies between the highest and lowest tide-marks. Now this would seem to be a very adequate definition as it clearly marks out the area. Unfortunately, these boundaries are not recognized by all of the animals and plants, for some undoubted shore organisms live much higher than the highest point reached by the tide. The upper limit for shore organisms appears to coincide with the highest point splashed by the breaking waves at high tide. For our purposes then, the shore is best defined as that part of the coast lying between the lowest tide mark and the highest point regularly reached by wave splash. The width of the shore is not constant; its extent is determined by the slope of the land and the size of the tide. Where the slope is steep and the tide small the shore is extremely narrow, where it is very gradual and the tide large the shore is very wide.

What causes the tide? Why do some places in the world have two tides a day and others only one? The tide is produced by the moon* and, to a lesser extent, the sun pulling at the surface of the sea, causing it to bulge (Figure 1). At the same time a second bulge is formed on the opposite side of the world because the force created by the rotation of our planet, which is slightly greater than the pull of the sun and moon on that same side, throws the sea outwards. These two bulges or tidal waves move round the earth as it turns raising the sea across the land

---

*Since the pull of the moon is the main tide-producing force the tides tend to have a 12·42 hour cycle, not a 12 hour one: the extra 25 minutes (50 minutes if only one tide per day) between successive tides is, of course, due to the change in position of the moon on its orbit around the earth.

13

wherever the two meet. There are then, nominally, two tides a day. The true picture, however, is not so simple (Figure 2). The land divides up the water covering our planet into compartments of different sizes, that is, into oceans, seas, gulfs, bays, channels, and in each of these one or several tidal bulges develop, each bulge rotating around a nodal point. The actual daily rhythm of the tide in a particular sea or channel will depend on size, shape and depth of the latter, for all of these affect the circular movement of a tidal bulge. New Zealand experiences that passage of a tidal bulge generated in two compartments of the sea, the South Western Pacific Basin and the Tasman and Coral Sea area. On both coasts there are two tides each day – the ideal rhythm. This is, however, hardly surprising since New Zealand lies alone in a vast expanse of deep sea and has a fairly straight coast and the tidal bulges move virtually unimpeded. In some parts of the world, e.g. the Gulf Mexico, there is only one tide each day; although the tide-generating force (the pull of the moon and sun) occurs twice a day it produces only a once-a-day cycle, this being the natural wave-movement for the body of water contained in that particulars compartment of the sea.

Each month, as the moon waxes and wanes, the size of the tide changes gradually from being very large to very small. The tides are small (NEAP) when the sun and moon pull against each other and large (SPRING) when they pull together.

The edge of the sea is motionless for only a fleeting moment when the tide turns on a very calm day. Most of the time it is restless, kept moving by the tide and waves. Waves are caused by the wind ruffling the surface of the sea. They may be very small, no more than the gentle rippling of the sea by a light breeze, or they may be large, either the sharp steep waves created by a local storm or the towering rollers formed by a hurricane far away on the other side of the ocean. When a wave breaks against the shore the tremendous energy contained in it is released; this energy is dissipated as the broken wave beats and tears at the surface of the shore. Great explosive forces are also produced as the air trapped by a curling wave is first compressed and then released. Breaking waves not only shape the shore, by smashing the rock or laying down sand, they also have a great effect on the organisms living on or in the shore, either directly as they crash against the bodies of those living on the surface of the rock or indirectly as they help to determine whether a beach is to be coarse or fine sediment.

You will know only too well that shores are not all the same; they may be of rock, shingle, sand or mud. Very rarely is the coast a continuous

14

line of any one of these, usually rocky platforms or cliffs are interrupted by boulder or sandy beaches. Harbours and river mouths make the structure of the coastline even more complicated. The coastline is fashioned by waves and currents; shores of rock are broken by waves and the pieces torn off are then gradually ground down into pebbles or sand grains which are eventually carried off by the currents to be laid down as a shingle bank or sandy beach somewhere further along the coast. Only in the most tranquil regions of a harbour or estuary do the finest particles (SILT) settle out on the bottom to form a mud flat.

It is now time to tell you about the plants and animals which live on different kinds of shore, particularly about where and how they live. Although at most places along the coast you will find rock and sand, or rock and mud, intermingled, they are best considered separately for each offers a very different sort of home. No more will be said about shingle for this is barren. The pebbles of a shingle beach are continually ground together by the breaking waves and anything rash enough to try to establish a home there would be quickly crushed.

Rocky Shores: Introduction

ZONATION: THE BASIC PATTERN

First let us look at the basic arrangement of animals and plants on the rocky shore. To introduce you to this arrangement we have chosen a man-made shore, a breakwater with a regular slope and fairly uniform surface, for it presents the pattern in its simplest form (Figure 3). The reason for doing this is that a regular natural shore is often hard to find. Most rocky shores are very irregular and so is the pattern of life – we will explain why later on.

By far the most striking feature about our artificial shore is that the organisms are arranged in bands. At the very lowest level the tide reaches is a belt of large brown seaweeds, a kelp (*Ecklonia radiata*) and the flapjack (*Carpophyllum maschalocarpum*). *Ecklonia* is fairly large, shiny and slippery and droops very characteristically when uncovered by the ebbing tide. The plant has three distinct parts: the attachment or holdfast, a cluster of radiating, branched, golden brown processes cemented to the rock; the long, flexible stalk or stipe, much darker in colour; and the large, much divided terminal blade, yellowish brown and often crinkled and frayed. The flapjack has quite a different appearance; it is tough and leathery; springing from the smallish root-like holdfast is the frond, a long, branched, dimpled strap with short, alternate side branches bearing long pointed 'leaves' and large elliptical bladders which float the plant when the tide is in.

Above the two browns are two bands of red seaweed, first a narrow zone of a purplish pink calcareous form, *Corallina officinalis*, and then a wider one of a small stubbly green (a red though it appears green to the naked eye) species, *Gelidium caulacantheum*. Heavily impregnated with lime, *Corallina* is rather gritty to feel; arising from the basal crust, the fronds, evenly branched towards the tip, are formed of jointed segments. *Gelidium caulacantheum* forms a loosely woven felt; the sinuous filaments branch irregularly and the short side-branches are curved and pointed.

About the middle of the shore is a zone of the rock oyster, *Crassostrea glomerata*, and above this a very wide fawn belt of the acorn barnacle,

16

Chamaesipho columna. Mis-shapen and jagged, the rock oysters are tightly packed together: the heavy shell, taking the shape of the space between its neighbours, is grey marked with fawn and brown and edged with black. It is the left valve of this tasty shellfish which is cemented to the rock; the young swimming stage or veliger larva instinctively attaches this side when it finally settles on the shore. The rock oyster feeds as it breathes, but only when covered by the tide. Cilia, tiny vibrating processes on the gills, draw a current of water in through the narrow opening between the valves of the shell and minute organisms and particles of debris floating in the sea are filtered out on the gills (long, filmy, perforated and folded membranes which partly encircle the muscle which closes the shell). The particles collected are conveyed to the paired, grooved, plate-like lips which sort out the smallest and pass them to the mouth. The current of water generated by the beating of the gill cilia leaves to the left of the hinge.

Chamaesipho columna is protected by a ring of fused calcareous plates shaped like a tiny volcano; the opening at the summit is guarded by two 'doors', each of two articulating plates. Like the rock oyster, *Chamaesipho columna* is often distorted by the growth of its neighbours. The acorn barnacle identifies itself as a crustacean when it sticks out its feathery jointed limbs to feed. The limbs form a net which is cast and withdrawn to catch small floating or swimming organisms when covered by the sea. A tough animal, like others of the upper shore, *Chamaesipho columna* will live after experiencing temperatures of over 45°C and below −5°C.

At the top of the breakwater the blocks of rock and the cement appear to be uninhabited. But if you look closely you will see that this part of the shore is occupied by a small snail, a periwinkle with a blue and cream banded shell (*Littorina unifasciata*), huddled in groups in crannies and depressions when the tide is out. The periwinkle shows itself when the surface of the rock is damp from wave splash or rain; the soft body is dark grey or black at the front, lighter and streaked behind. *Littorina unifasciata* feeds on diatoms and the sporelings of seaweeds and lichens which are scraped off the rock with the toothed tongue. For an animal which has not quite broken its bond with the sea (it produces swimming young and has a tiny gill), it is extremely hardy; *Littorina* will survive after suffering temperatures up to 45°C, the loss of more than half of the water in its body, and submersion in freshwater (for a week or more).

Above the highest level reached by the tide the blocks are daubed, here and there, with patches of orange 'paint', a lichen called *Xanthoria*

17

parietina. A plant of this lichen is often circular in outline, with irregular radiating ridges and simply branched finger-like projections at the edge, and the central region covered with disc-shaped fruiting bodies. For those who do not know, a lichen is an unusual plant; it is a mixture of green algal cells and fungal filaments.

This pattern of zones of organisms will be a feature of the rocky shore wherever you go along the coast. It will always be there, though at times it will not be very obvious because of the irregular nature of the rock.

THE CAUSES OF ZONATION AND OF ITS VARIATION

Before looking at some natural shores and the animals and plants which live on them, you will, we are sure, want to ask some questions about the pattern of life on the breakwater. Important amongst many questions will be the following. Why is it that only certain sea organisms live on the shore? Why do some of them live higher on the shore than others? Why are the zones of sedentary animals and plants so even? It is difficult to answer any one of them simply, for the nature of life on the shore, or for that matter in any habitat, be it a pond or the bush, is very complex. The relationships between animals and plants and between them and their environment are intricate, more so than any mechanism devised by man. No one thing seems to absolutely control another; test this for yourself by following what happens when you clear a small area of barnacles, or limpets and top shells, or oyster borers, or anything else. However often you repeat the experiment the events which follow the removal of the organisms will never be exactly the same. You will appreciate that there is a balance between the species which live in a particular place on the shore. The point of balance is continually shifting as the structure of this group of species (the community) changes because of the birth, growth and death of individuals or by the action of the sea or air. You can see the shift in balance for yourself if you remove a prominent member-species of the community and prevent it from re-establishing itself.

You may have already realized that the seashore is a most inhospitable place to make a home. Twice a day the tide ebbs and flows across the shore. At low water animals and plants on the shore are at the mercy of the weather; chilled and soaked with rain on a wet day in winter and dried and heated on a windy, sunny day in summer. These are the

18

extremes and most days during the year will not be quite so exacting. The plants and animals have to withstand the rigours of the atmosphere until the tide returns to wet them again. Now, although the return of the sea relieves the stress caused by exposure to the air, it also brings other problems. The quality and strength of the sunlight is altered by having to penetrate the water; this is very important since light is used by the seaweeds to make food. The rising tide brings back the waves and also allows grazing and predacious animals such as limpets and rock shells to be active again.

Naturally you will wonder what enables an organism to endure such sharp changes in the weather each day. You will probably look at their structure for the answer. Most true shore organisms are robustly built; the seaweeds, barnacles, snails, chitons, rock-oyster are very tough, often heavily built – the animals are generally squat and the plants have very strong holdfasts. But this is only part of the answer – the rest of it lies in their peculiar behaviour and very different 'internal make-up' or constitution (this cannot be seen – it must be tested in the laboratory). Every organism is a precision machine, very delicately adjusted to operate correctly in certain conditions. Shore organisms have an 'internal make-up' which enables them to function in widely fluctuating climatic conditions.

It is also the 'internal make-up' which permits some shore organisms to live higher than others. We have just explained that this is specially adapted for life on the shore. In each kind of shore animal and plant the 'internal make-up' is set differently and therefore there are as many different abilities to cope with the continually changing shore climate as there are species. Some are better adapted than others and can thus live higher; a few have been adjusted so much in one direction as to actually dislike continuous immersion in the sea. Try keeping large periwinkles submerged in a dish of sea-water.

Does the dislike of prolonged submergence determine the lower limit of an organism living on the shore? In some cases, for example some seaweeds, the top shells, limpets and periwinkles, it does play a large part, but it is seldom the sole cause. With sedentary animals like the barnacles and the rock oyster competition for space with other organisms sets this limit; specialized habits, grazing by herbivorous snails and limpets, predation by rock shells, welks and starfish are all very important too.

Straight zonal boundaries occur where an organism's upper or lower limit is reached, or where there is an even struggle for living space between two adjacent species, or where the activities of grazers and predators are intense. In the defence of its zone, a sedentary animal, such as a barnacle, is greatly aided by the young settling where the adults already live and filling up the vacant spaces. Mobile animals, like the limpets and top shells, have definite upper and lower limits, but these are not immediately obvious.

You will go to many rocky shores and see zonation, and knowing that the tide has regular monthly and annual cycles, will wonder whether this orderly pattern has anything to do with the tides. Sometimes you will discover that the boundary between two zones coincides with a certain tidal level, for example MEAN LOW-WATER NEAPS, but more often it does not. The shore is a very complex environment with its two climates, that of the sea and of the air. It is the adaptation of the organism to the whole of its environment which matters, not just to separate parts of it. A single factor can, however, alter the picture. Take waves as an example; waves have a double effect, they smash with great force against the shore and as they do, spray is thrown high up, often well beyond the highest tidal mark, keeping the rock very wet there. The force and the wetting effect of the waves increase as one moves from a sheltered to an exposed shore. You will discover that the zones are gradually raised and that the species change. The spray from the breaking waves pushes the upper limit of the shore well beyond the highest mark reached by the tide (our definition of the shore recognizes this). The species composing the zonal pattern change because of their different tolerances to sea-surface conditions – some prefer still water, others rough.

Other parts of the shore climate also greatly modify the zonal pattern by causing a change of occupant or the height of the zones. Some of these agents produce readily observed effects and these should be looked for when you examine a particular shore. Freshwater either as a stream running across the reef or as a river will exclude all but the few organisms e.g. the green seaweed *Enteromorpha intestinalis*, the barnacle *Elminius modestus* which can cope with dilute conditions. The orientation of the reef has considerable influence; whilst a north face becomes warm and dry at low tide, a south face remains cool and wet and promotes the upward extension of many organisms: a gradual slope remaining wet because it drains slowly when the tide ebbs will have the same effect. The nature of the rock causes differences; on a soft, easily eroded mudstone limpets are dominant, on a hard, resistant granite they give way to barnacles. Sand in the water scours and smothers; rock swept by

20

water loaded with sand is occupied only by those organisms capable of withstanding such conditions or which need the sand for building a tube e.g. the bristle worm *Sabellaria kaiparaensis*.

MAIN ZONES OF THE ROCKY SHORE

As yet we have little information of a precise sort about the influences which cause individual zonal boundaries. There certainly seems to be, as far as one can see, no relationship between many of the zonal boundaries and significant differences, at the same level on the shore, of any of the individual parts (e.g. the tide) of the environment which can be measured accurately. Here the boundaries must result from the complex interplay of certain components of the environment, but, unfortunately we have yet to find some means of estimating this interplay. However, there are four boundaries which seem to be associated with marked changes (over a year) in the duration of drying and heating and these can be employed to divide the rocky shore into three basic zones (indicated by certain organisms). The reality of these four boundaries seems confirmed by the occurrence of these three zones on most shores of the world.

The three life zones of the rocky shore are: (1) the lower shore (indicated by large brown seaweeds such as the kelp *Ecklonia radiata* or the bull kelp *Durvillea antarctica*, encrusting calcareous red seaweeds, corals, sponges or sea-squirts) is the region of the shore which is uncovered only briefly for a few days each month i.e. during spring tides but never dries out completely – the lower boundary on sheltered shores lies at EXTREME LOW WATER SPRINGS and the upper boundary may lie close to AVERAGE LOW TIDAL LEVEL (a tidal point about which there is a rapid change in the total time, taken over a year, of submersion or, conversely, emersion), on exposed shores these boundaries are raised, the upper quite considerably, by the swash and splash of the breaking waves; (2) the middle shore (indicated by acorn barnacles such as *Chamaesipho columna*, though often the barnacles share the rock with other sessile organisms e.g. tube worms, the rock oyster) is the region of the shore covered and uncovered completely or almost completely by the sea every day – the upper boundary may coincide with AVERAGE HIGH TIDAL LEVEL (another tidal point about which there is a rapid change in the amount of submersion to emersion) in harbours, but on the open coast it is raised to a higher level (well above EXTREME

HIGH WATER SPRINGS in exposed places) by the swash and splash of the breaking waves; and (3) the upper shore (indicated by periwinkles such as *Littorina unifasciata*, black lichens and blue-green algae) is the region of the shore which is wetted by the sea for only a short part of each month – on sheltered shores it is wetted only at spring tides (the upper boundary approximates to EXTREME HIGH WATER SPRINGS), on exposed shores it is wetted when the rock is splashed by the breaking waves, mainly at high tide (the upper boundary is well above EXTREME HIGH WATER SPRINGS).

Two Natural Shores

We now describe two natural rocky shores. One is from the east coast where it lies at the entrance of a harbour, protected from the full force of the Pacific Ocean by a peninsula and islands; the other is from the west coast facing into the prevailing wind and huge Tasman rollers. Both shores are of volcanic rock which is very hard and rough and forms a good firm surface for the attachment of organisms. A quick look at the drawings of these shores show that the animals and plants are zoned, just as they are on the breakwater. But the zonation of these shores differs from that of the breakwater and from each other. Firstly, the pattern is not nearly so neat and tidy; the reason for this is the unevenness of the rock surface; there are nooks and crannies, flat surfaces facing different directions, angular parts, all creating different living conditions. It is seldom that you will find a natural shore with an even pattern like that of our breakwater, for the coast rarely wears to an even surface and regular slope because of the varying nature of the rock and abrading forces (waves, wind, sand and stones).

On the east coast shore (Figure 5) the zoning organisms are much the same as those of the breakwater, except that a tube worm (*Pomatoceros caeruleus*) has established a narrow zone below the rock oyster. *Pomatoceros* is a bristle worm which lives permanently in a white, tapered, calcareous tube, triangular in section with a prominent keel projecting as a short, sharp spine above the opening. When covered by the sea, the animal protrudes its crown of feathery plumes or gills, blackish blue with narrow bars of white. The crown, formed of two separate semi-circles of plumes, is the feeding organ and the main respiratory surface. Cilia, in discrete tracts, create a current of water which passes between the plumes into the central space and then upwards and out. Particles, tiny organisms and detritus, are trapped in mucus and conveyed to the base of the crown and sorted there, the finest are ingested and the rest rejected into outgoing water current. You cannot help but notice that *Pomatoceros* is a master of the disappearing act; withdrawal into the tube is instantaneous if you tap the rock with your foot or pass your shadow across the crown. Like the rock oyster and barnacle, the hard 'house' of the individual, in this case the tube, can be moulded to fit irregular and restricted spaces. Also, there is a lower zone of barnacles (*Elminius modestus*) instead of a little stubbly red seaweed. There is a slight raising of the zones too since this shore is a little more exposed to the waves than is the breakwater.

On the west coast shore (Figure 6), which is also volcanic though of a different formation (a breccia, with large sharp fragments set in a 'cement' of finer particles), many of the zoning organisms are different from those of the east coast shore and of the breakwater. The barnacles and periwinkle met before are present here, but they are accompanied in force by some of their close relatives. The second periwinkle (*Littorina cincta*), though similar in body colour, has a shell lined with brown and it grows to a larger size. *Littorina cincta* obviously has a liking for heavy waves for it is the dominant periwinkle on very exposed rocky shores, particularly to the south. There are two barnacles in addition to the small species already met with on the eastern shores. One of these (*Chamaesipho brunnea*) is a very close relative for it has the ivory plates of its test or shell welded together. It is, however, squat and much bigger and only occurs (on this particular part of the coast) in small groups. *Chamaesipho brunnea* seems to love the pounding surf for on the wildest stretches of the coast it completely replaces the little *C. columna*. On moderately exposed rocky shores *Chamaesipho brunnea* is restricted to the upper part of the barnacle belt (it is more resistant to desiccation than *C. columna*); it is not very successful in competition with *Chamaesipho columna* which crowds it out from below. At a lower level *Chamaesipho columna* is helped by the activities of the carnivorous snails, the oyster borer *Lepsiella scobina* and the rock shell *Neothais scalaris*, which prefer the larger *C. brunnea*. The other barnacle (*Elminius plicatus*) is also fairly large and lives in little clusters, but its four, cream and pale yellow, strongly ribbed plates are quite free. Lying between the periwinkle and barnacle zones is a narrow band of the red seaweed *Bostrychia arbuscula*, the fine, pointed and evenly branched filaments giving a nap to the rock. Seaweeds also form broken belts at the top and bottom of the barnacle zone. At the top you will find the pale purple tissue paper-like rosettes of karengo (*Porphyra columbina*), a primitive red seaweed, and at the bottom are clumps of the channelled-wrack (*Gigartina alveata*) with narrow drooping branches, divided and curled at the tips. Below the mixed barnacle – channelled wrack belt is a broad zone of the green and black mussel (*Perna canaliculus*), much

24

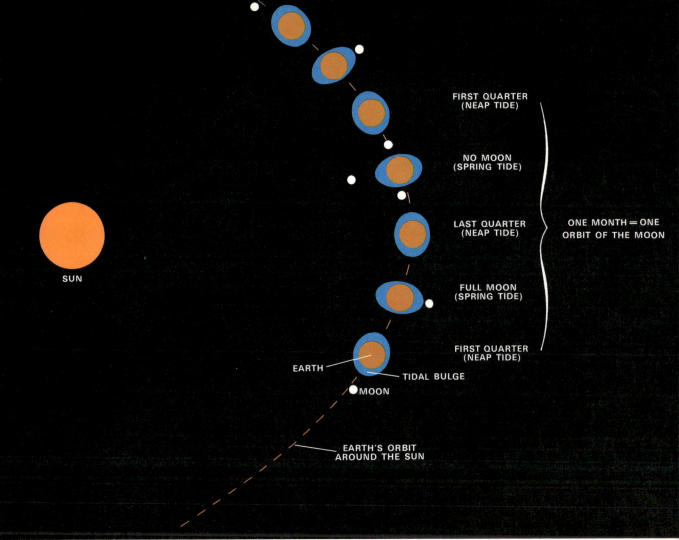

FIRST QUARTER
(NEAP TIDE)

NO MOON
(SPRING TIDE)

LAST QUARTER
(NEAP TIDE)

FULL MOON
(SPRING TIDE)

FIRST QUARTER
(NEAP TIDE)

ONE MONTH = ONE
ORBIT OF THE MOON

SUN

EARTH

TIDAL BULGE

MOON

EARTH'S ORBIT
AROUND THE SUN

1. A simple picture of the attractive forces of the Moon and Sun causing the tide on an Earth completely covered by water of a uniform depth. The Sun and Moon (the stronger force) pull on the layer of water (oceans and seas) causing it to bulge (the tidal wave). A similar bulge is also formed on the opposite side; this one is caused by the water tending to be thrown outwards by the spinning Earth. During one full turn of the Earth any one locality will experience the passage of both of these bulges or tidal waves (giving two high and low tides each day). The bulges (tidal waves) are largest when the Sun and Moon pull together (full and new moon), at other phases of the lunar month the bulges are smaller, being smallest when the Sun and Moon pull on the Earth at right angles to each other (first and third quarter of the lunar month). In reality such bulges, called progressive waves, are not formed; instead, because the sea is divided up by the land, several waves are formed. Also, the wave is of a different sort (called a stationary wave, see 2).

2. The tide as a stationary wave (a tilting of the sea surface which is caused by the pull of the Sun and Moon). A better known example of a stationary wave is the slopping movement of soup in a bowl or tea in a cup as it is carried about (see diagram B).

A. A map of the Pacific Ocean showing the centres and movements (mainly rotatory, caused by the spin of the Earth) of the stationary waves which cause the tide; the lines join places which experience high tide at the same time and the numbers indicate times of high tide in hours (lunar) after the transit of the Moon at Greenwich. New Zealand lies roughly at the centre of a stationary wave which rotates anticlockwise; this wave is produced by the two adjacent tidal waves, one in the Coral-Tasman Sea area, the other in the South Western Pacific Basin, which rotate clockwise (the normal direction for a wave generated in the Southern Hemisphere). The size of the tide lessens gradually to zero at the point (nodal or amphidromic) around which the stationary wave revolves.

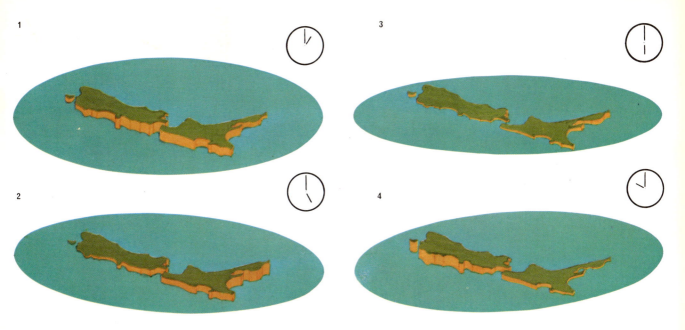

B. A series of diagrams demonstrating the circular movement of the stationary wave in the compartment of the sea containing New Zealand. The time differences in high tide (or any other tidal state) between places along the coast result from the gradual passage of this wave.

CAPTION FOR FIG. 5 (OVERLEAF)

5. Zones of animals and plants on a shore of basalt facing NE. at the entrance to a harbour on the East coast of the North Island and subject to moderate waves. The pattern of zones is uneven and broken due mainly to the irregular nature of the rock surface.

EHWS — EXTREME HIGH WATER SPRINGS, ELWS — EXTREME LOW WATER SPRINGS. Extreme tidal range — 3·7m (12 feet).
2–4, 6 and 8 as in figure 3.

5. *Pomatoceros caerulens*, a tube worm forming a narrow zone where the rock face is steep. 5a, a small group of worms, all but one with the crown of feathery breathing-feeding tentacles protruded from the calcareous tube.
7. *Codium adhaerens*, a green seaweed (see figure 3). 7a, a small plant.
9. *Elminius modestus*, a small barnacle (see figure 10). 9a, a small group. Rarely larger than 5 mm. across.
10. *Ecklonia radiata*, a kelp which is very characteristic of reefs in sheltered waters; most plants are partly submerged even at the lowest tide. 10a, one plant. Length up to 1 m.

Figure 5

5a

9a

10a

7a

EHWS ▶

2

3

4

5

7

9

6

ELWS ▶

8

10

fancied by local gourmands and the large pink or purple reef star (*Stichaster australis*). The mussel, though attached to the rock like the rock oyster and feeding in the same way, is not permanently fixed; the animal can release its fastening, the group of golden radiating threads (the byssus), and draw itself along with the very mobile and extensible foot, chocolate brown in colour like the edge of the cloak which protrudes from the shell. When the mussel is feeding you will notice that the edge of the cloak has two distinct parts, a frill along most of the opening, the entrance for the respiratory and feeding current, and a very short, incomplete tube (the siphon), the exit. *Stichaster* (Figure 7), the mussel's enemy, is rough and rigid. You will need a strong, flat implement to prise it from the rock; the tube feet, the organs of crawling and attachment, are stuck to the rock so firmly that many are broken when the starfish is pulled off the rock. As the tide comes in *Stichaster* moves up to feed on *Perna*; it turns its stomach inside out and inserts it into the shell through the narrow gap where the byssus passes between the two valves, and digests the soft parts. On occasion *Stichaster* will feed on *Chamaesipho columna*; clumps of this barnacle are torn off with the tube feet and enwrapped with the stomach. The lowest level is dominated by seaweeds, or sponges in fairly protected gullies. The surface of the rock, where it is visible, is daubed with pink 'paint', a calcareous red seaweed (*Lithothamnium*). Foremost here is the bull kelp (*Durvillea antarctica*); this is an enormous seaweed, sometimes reaching a length of 30 feet or more, with a large light yellow holdfast (the disc which fastens the plant to the rock) about the size of a small omelette, a short, narrow, blond stem and a large flattened, rubbery, sepia frond, cut deeply into thongs of varying lengths and widths. The frond of a large plant has air spaces which keep it afloat.

More about Life on Open Rock

We have told you about the basic pattern of life on open rock, how it is altered by wave action, surface irregularity and latitude. In our description of this pattern a few of the common zone forming organisms have been named and something said about how some of the animals maintain themselves in such an inhospitable place. But we cannot leave this part of the shore yet. There are many other organisms living in the open which you will encounter on most of your walks along the rocky shore. We must tell you about some of them.

SEAWEEDS AND THEIR RELATIVES

How do seaweeds, seemingly delicate plants, withstand exposure to the sun and wind? They do not show any of the adaptations of desert plants against desiccation, such as water storing stems and reduced evaporating surfaces such as the spines (instead of leaves). How do they resist the tearing action of the waves? The explanations lie partly in their architecture and partly in their internal functioning.

Seaweeds are simple in structure – they possess none of the complex tissues of flowering plants. They do not even have supporting tissue, for when the tide retreats they just flop over on to the rock. However, this apparent droopiness is a real advantage: it is essential for seaweeds to be supple for they must bend with the water flow created by waves and currents when immersed. Anyway, this droopiness does not mean weakness – try tearing even a small seaweed from the surface of the rock, usually the frond tears before the 'root' (holdfast) is detached or the 'stalk' (stipe) snaps. The holdfast forms a very strong bond with the rock – there is dove-tailing between the cells of the holdfast and the minute irregularities of the rock surface and a film of gluey substance is secreted. The cell walls of the core of these lowest parts of the plant are very thick, also the cells are arranged in alternating courses like the bricks of a wall, a form of building which combines strength and flexibility. Added strength is imparted by long processes which grow out of and between the cells to form a reinforcing network within the stipe and holdfast. At the holdfast some of these processes may even grow outwards to form a further connection with the rock. These filaments tend to grow downwards and thus form a crude pathway for the transport of food substances. The frond is weaker; the reason for this is that the bending moments created by the movement of the sea are not so severe since mobility is increased further away from the point of attachment (the holdfast). A large, flattened blade is theoretically the simplest type of frond for a water plant; it is flexible, it offers a large surface for catching light and absorbing mineral salts and no part is far from the food making surface. Few living seaweeds have, however, a frond of this shape; usually it is much divided thus offering an even greater surface for photosynthesis and mineral salt absorption and much less resistance to water movement since the several parts can bend differentially to the complex eddying of the water. This is very much the case with seaweeds living in very rough waters – even our largest and toughest species, *Durvillea antarctica*, has a finely divided frond. This does not mean that all seaweeds have large divided fronds and well developed stipes; when later we look at some of our seaweeds you will see that other frond shapes have been adopted.

How do soft, unprotected plants like seaweeds prevent drying out when the ebbing tide subjects them to the sun and wind? This must be a serious problem, especially for those seaweeds living near the top of the shore. Seaweeds reduce water loss in several ways; they produce mucilage, a gummy substance secreted by all seaweeds, they have cells with thick walls (exceedingly so in species living in the top half of the shore). Both contain water and it is this water which is given up first. When, however, all of the water has been removed from the mucilage and cell walls, it is then drawn off from inside the cells. Loss of water does not impair the functioning of many seaweeds living on the shore, for they have an internal 'make-up' which enables them to function during such stress. You will find, not surprisingly, that species of seaweed living high on the shore are better adapted to water loss than those lower down. Some seaweeds of the upper reaches of the shore have become so well adapted to living in air that they will tolerate losing nearly two-thirds of their water; in fact, it has been shown that they will not live if continually immersed. They can photosynthesize in both the air and water.

Other environmental factors are important; temperature is one. Again the seaweeds of the open surface are remarkably well adapted; some of

27

the species of the upper part of the shore can withstand temperatures above 35°C and below –10°C (even to having three quarters of their water content converted to ice). Light is another: some high level species become adjusted to photosynthesizing in such bright light that they cannot do it in the dim light of submergence.

There are four groups of seaweeds, principally classified on their colour – blue-green, green, brown and red. Colour is not, unfortunately, a reliable basis for identification; some of the reds are brown or dark purple and some of the browns are olive green. The reds are the biggest group and show the greatest range of shape; many of the small, delicate species are very difficult for the beginner to identify. We must warn you that although seaweed structure is simple, the reproductive bodies and life-histories are complicated.

It is now time to describe some of the other common seaweeds of open rock. Few seaweeds live at the top of the shore. Those that do are mostly blue-greens. One common species is *Calothrix scopulorum* (Figure 8.1), which takes the form of a thin, olive green mat of minute threads. Each thread consists of a single row of cells bound in a gelatinous sheath. Two other seaweeds are commonly found at the same level, but only in winter when the air is cool and the rock remains moist. One of these is a green seaweed, *Enteromorpha compressa*, which consists of long, branched tubular fronds arising from a minute disc-like holdfast (Figure 8.4); it is particularly abundant where fresh water trickles across the shore. The other is *Scytosiphon lomentaria* (Figure 9.3), a small brown seaweed which looks not unlike *Enteromorpha*, but the fronds are not branched and are usually constricted at regular intervals like a string of sausages, and they are pale olive brown and rather slimy.

In contrast the middle shore is well dotted with seaweeds of quite a wide variety. Most obvious is the sea lettuce, *Ulva lactuca*, which has the form of thin but tough transparent sheets, bright to dark green in colour, radiating from a tiny disc-shaped holdfast (Figure 8.2). The sea lettuce is particularly common just above and amongst the green mussel on exposed coasts. The brown seaweeds are very prominent here and show a wide array of very distinctive forms. High on this part of the shore is *Scytothamnus australis* (Figure 9.5), an untidy plant rather like a wind swept leafless tree or the business end of a witch's broom, coffee to olive in colour, set here and there amongst the barnacles in fairly exposed places. A little further down the shore occurs the gummy weed, *Splachnidium rugosum* (Figure 9.2), with its tough, wrinkled, olive to dark brown skin and fat club-like branches filled with mucilage which

28

are attached to the rock by a small conical holdfast. Neptune's necklace, *Hormosira banksii* (Figure 10.1), is the most famous of our seaweeds; it occurs in fairly quiet waters and often carpets the middle of the shore. The frond consists of long branched strings of pimply beads (gas filled, oxygen during the day and carbon dioxide during the night), usually olive brown in colour, attached to the rock by a small disc. The 'beads' or bladders, and consequently the whole plant, are large in backwaters and small where the wave action is fairly strong. *Hormosira* is truly a seaweed of the shore for it can not only tolerate the loss of 60% of its water, but will continue to photosynthesize when uncovered by the retreating sea. At roughly the same level on the shore, and where the rock is hard and smooth, you will find an encrusting species; *Ralfsia verrucosa* (Figure 8.9) has the form of leathery, rather brittle, olive brown to sepia, circular patches, lumpy in the centre and marked with circular and radiating lines. Adjacent plants of this seaweed as they grow, coalesce where they touch to form large irregular patches. Here too occurs two other kinds of compacted, though hollow, seaweed. *Leathesia difformis* (Figure 9.1) is roughly hemispherical, much folded, thick-walled and shiny, and is slippery to touch and honey-yellow in colour. *Colpomenia sinuosa* (Figure 9.4) is more or less spherical when young, but becomes lobed when old; it is thin-walled, smooth and matt, yellow to olive green in colour. At the lowest level of the middle part of the shore in places of moderate to strong wave action occurs *Xiphophora chondrophylla* (Figure 9.6), a brown which has a frond of long, evenly branched, thick straps, rather leathery and olive-green in colour; the holdfast is a circle of thick 'roots' (haptera). Very few red seaweeds live on open rock in the upper or middle reaches of the shore. *Bostrychia arbuscula*, mentioned in an earlier section, is one of the few; *Apophloea sinclairii* (Figure 10.4) is another. *Apophloea* occurs as dull red, cartilaginous patches, sometimes produced into short, upright, branched processes. On a hot day, when the tide is out, the plants lose a lot of their water and consequently become very shrivelled and dry looking, rather like patches of dried blood.

On the lowest part of the shore the seaweeds are luxuriant. We have already described several of the most obvious forms viz. *Durvillea*, *Carpophyllum* and *Ecklonia*, all of them brown seaweeds. However, we must mention here one other brown, a most striking looking kind called *Glossophora kunthii*, so common on gently sloping reefs exposed to fairly strong wave action. *Glossophora* (Figure 8.7) has a frond regularly divided into straps with a nap of small membranous outgrowths, giving it a

29

tongue-like appearance; the frond is olive and the stipe coffee in colour. Here the red seaweeds are very common and diverse, so much so, that we can only mention three species, all common and easily recognizable. *Melanthalia abscissa* (Figure 10.6) has a frond of narrow, stiff, very regularly divided branches, dark red when wet, almost black when dry. *Liagora harveyana* (Figure 10.2) is a short plant of narrow, cylindrical, evenly divided branches, slightly calcified though soft, and slippery to touch, white near the base becoming pink then reddish brown towards the tips; it forms a thick turf on shores where there is moderate wave action. Finally, *Plocamium costatum* (Figure 10.5) which has a frond of narrow, flattened branches, the regularly spaced curved and pointed side branches giving it the appearance of a double edged, coarsely toothed, saw blade; it is bright red.

There are other plants on the shore, very close relatives of the seaweeds (they belong to the same group, the Algae), but they are so small as to be invisible to the naked eye. They are the diatoms, dinoflagellates and microflagellates, little plants which are so abundant in the surface layers of the sea. Some of these tiny plants live permanently in places which remain damp, others are lodged on the shore with splash from the waves.

Like the green land plants, the seaweeds and their minute relatives are the producers of food (for themselves and the animals); using the sun's energy, carbon dioxide (aided by salts and water) is converted into complex substances. It is the delicate sporelings and the minute forms (diatoms, dinoflagellates and microflagellates) which contribute immediately to the economy of the shore, for they are eaten by many animals. Large seaweeds, although eaten by a few grazing animals, make their contribution as detritus produced by death and decay.

ANIMALS

Now to the commoner animals of open rock. First, there are two sedentary animals, both particularly widespread. One is *Elminius modestus* (Figures 5 and 11), a small, white, star shaped barnacle which lives on rock in harbours and estuaries, and under stones on more exposed coasts (it will also live on wharf piles and a ship's hull). The other is a tiny black mussel, *Xenostrobus pulex* (Figure 12), which like its relatives, prefers living with its own kind and often forms a pure carpet along the middle of the shore. When the shell gapes the two openings to the gill cavity are obvious and somewhat different in form and extent to

11. A group of *Elminius modestus*, a little barnacle easily recognized by the four distinct, lobed, body plates which give it a star-like shape. It lives in harbours and the mouths of estuaries on open rock, snail shells, wharf piles and the aerial roots and trunk of the mangrove; on more open shores it occurs on the under surfaces of stones at a low level on the shore. *E. modestus* fouls the bottoms of ships and has been carried to European waters where it is spreading.

those of *Perna canaliculus*; the entry for the water current is indicated by two rows, one on each side, of short, branched, sensory processes (these test the in-coming water) and the exit is short and trumpet-shaped, weakly digitate at the edge. These extensions of the cloak (the mantle) are purple at the base grading to pale orange brown at the extremities. Both openings are at the large (hind) end of the body. *Xenostrobus* collects and sorts the food in the same way as *Perna canaliculus* and *Crassostrea glomerata*. *Xenostrobus* is very hardy for it likes heavy wave action and does not mind being buried temporarily under sand. The rest are all mobile animals. None of them is common enough to form an obvious band, but they are zoned. Each kind has upper and lower limits beyond which it seldom wanders.

The large shore crab, *Leptograpsus variegatus* (Figure 13), lives on the upper half of the shore: it is strong, agile and runs swiftly. It has long spiny legs with curved and pointed claws which enable it to maintain a good grip whilst running quickly over the uneven rock. It is a very nervous creature and is very easily disturbed – it retreats rapidly beneath boulders or into large fissures and wedges itself so tightly as to resist the most strenuous efforts to dislodge it. It is recognized by having a body that is obliquely grooved and finely toothed along the front margin. Large animals are usually dark reddish brown and fawn, smaller ones are mauve. The pincers are white and deep magenta and covered with tubercles. *Leptograpsus* is much more able to cope with land conditions than most other crabs of our shores. During ebb tide it loses water to the atmosphere, but its internal 'make-up' is adapted to working under such conditions; it certainly does not seem to affect this animal's activity. The salt content of this crab's blood is lower than seawater, therefore when the animal is covered by the sea it loses water, though the speed of loss is reduced by special processes going on inside its body. Fresh-water, in the form of rain, has an effect, though the opposite, for water invades the body – the animal has some control over the rate of ingress. *Leptograpsus* shows little concern for a strict diet, eagerly devouring dead animals and seaweeds, lodged high on the shore by the waves or left there by the receding tide, as well as living seaweeds, snails, worms and other small animals.

Prominent along the middle of the shore, in sheltered and fairly exposed places, is the snakeskin chiton, *Sypharochiton pelliserpentis* (Figure 14). It is a largish chiton, protected by its eight piece shell, often eroded and grey to dirty brown in colour, and skirt of small scales, fawn broken by thick bars of dark brown. Being low and very flexible, *Sypharochiton* can occupy all sorts of narrow and irregular crannies, places which large snails with tall and rigid shells cannot enter. When the tide is out this chiton sits snugly and tightly in a depression, its 'scar' or 'home'. When the tide is in it roams the surrounding rock, returning to its 'scar' when the tide recedes. *Sypharochiton*, like *Leptograpsus*, has some control over water movement in and out of its body. In this case, however, it is not an internal mechanism: all the chiton does is draw itself tightly against the rock, thereby reducing contact between the more permeable under-parts of the body and the surrounding dilute medium. Its kidneys also bale out much of the inflowing water. Not surprisingly, *Sypharochiton* can also tolerate a considerable loss of water from its body and quite high temperatures, at least 35°C.

Snails are a very prominent feature of the open rock. We have already discussed the periwinkles which are so characteristic of the uppermost level of the shore, but what of the many other snails. The limpets – these are indeed snails though their shells are conical – are described first. Most obvious of these are the true limpets, *Cellana ornata* (Figure 15) with its brown and white striped, heavily ridged shell and cream body, and *Cellana radians* (Figure 16) with a low, faintly ridged shell, marked with a broken brown network, and bluish grey body. Both of these limpets move about the rock when covered by the tide or on a humid or wet night when the tide is out. Like the snakeskin chiton, *Cellana ornata* has a 'scar' or 'home' (*Cellana radians* does not) to which it returns after a feeding excursion; it usually makes a circular tour, seldom returning by the same path. The circuit is usually made down the shore at night with the tide out and up the shore when in. There are two questions to be asked here. How does it navigate? Why does the limpet home? Unfortunately, though answers to these questions have long

32

been sought, we still do not know. All we can say is that the direction of the light rays, chemicals or a memory of the local rock surface alone do not seem to be the primary means of determining the route to be taken by the animal. As to the second question; it is suggested that the 'home' is a place on the shore where the limpet is more secure in the competition for living space, and against predators and drying out. Conservation of water could well be the principal reason for having a 'home'; *Cellana ornata*, which possesses a 'home', lives higher on the shore than *Cellana radians* and may well need an additional means of reducing water loss. Even without the 'home', *Cellana ornata* seems well adapted to long periods of wind and sun, for it can tolerate the loss of up to 60% of its water (nearly twice the tolerance shown by *C. radians*) and a temperature of 40°C. *Cellana ornata* does not completely outshine *C. radians* as a shore animal, for the latter can cope with soft rock, turbid water and sand scour, conditions which usually exclude the former species. Two other limpets which occur commonly are *Notoacmea pileopsis* and *Notoacmea parviconoidea*. *Notoacmea pileopsis* (Figure 17) lives on shaded vertical faces at the top of exposed shores; the shell is smooth, dull brown flecked with white, and the animal is uniformly fawn. The other acmaeid limpet, *Notoacmea parviconoidea* (Figure 18), lives amongst the barnacles; it is small and the shell is eroded and grey at the top and a band of brown and grey stripes around the bottom. The body is light grey and the head is tinged with pink. Both of these limpets home accurately.

15. *Cellana ornata*, the ornate limpet, another of our larger limpet species; it is common on the surface of reefs and boulders of hard rock in the upper half of the middle shore. Length up to 32 mm.

16. *Cellana radians*, the radiate limpet, is common on boulders and reefs in the lower half of the middle shore on most rocky coasts. Length up to 44 mm.

17. *Notoacmea pileopsis*, a limpet which is very characteristic of the upper shore (along with the periwinkles) and upper reaches of the middle shore on rocky coasts exposed to heavy waves. It is not always easy to identify since the shell of individuals which live amongst the barnacles is often slightly mis-shapen and eroded. This limpet moves about feeding on humid nights when the tide is out. Length up to 28 mm.

There are many snails with coiled shells on the open rock, three of the commonest being the black nerite, *Nerita melanotragus*, the black top shell, *Melagraphia aethiops*, and the cat's eye, *Lunella smaragda*. The black nerite (Figure 19) is dome-shaped, matt black with a pure white aperture, which, when the animal, also black, withdraws inside, is stoppered with a curved golden brown 'door' (operculum). It lives throughout the upper two-thirds of the middle shore and retreats to pools or huddles together, often in very large groups, in crannies or on moist surfaces, when the tide is out. Several explanations have been offered for these congregations; they may help reduce the loss of water from the young or keep their temperature down, or they may act as dispersal centres (the older individuals leaving a group as the young join it) or as protection against the waves. Although very resistant to low or high temperatures, water loss, cloudy water and dilution of the sea, *Nerita* is not good at hanging on to the rock and perhaps because of this it is not able to occupy open rock where the waves are of more than a moderate size. The black top shell (Figure 20), which is really purple

18. *Notoacmea parviconoidea*, a tiny limpet of rocky coasts suffering moderate wave action; it lives amongst barnacles and the little black mussel, *Xenostrobus pulex*. Like *Notoacmea pileopsis*, it is not always easy to identify by its brown banded shell since the upper two-thirds or so is often eroded to a pale grey. Length up to 9 mm.

19. *Nerita melanotragus*, the black nerite. This snail is a very common occupant, sometimes forming groups of a hundred or more, of the middle shore of reefs and boulders not subject to heavy waves. *Nerita* moves about feeding during the day and night, even at low tide when the rock is still moist. It is a pool dweller too, usually congregating about the water-line; in pools it penetrates into the upper shore zone. Failure in competition with the cat's eye seems to be the reason for the absence of the black nerite from the lower shore. Confined to the North Island, *Nerita melanotragus* is rather scarce on the West coast and in the south. Height (of the shell) up to 30 mm.

and black, has a very characteristic white checked pattern; the upper whorls are eroded and pearly and the operculum is circular (as in all top shells) and dark brown. The body is yellowish green heavily overlaid with black. *Melagraphia* lives on the same sort of shores as *Nerita*, but is not nearly as common and is restricted to the lower part of the middle shore since it is not very tolerant of water loss. It is a fast moving snail and wanders about extensively and randomly within its narrow zone of operation. Like *Nerita*, *Melagraphia* is poor at clinging to the rock and therefore avoids heavy waves. The cat's eye (Figure 21) is a fairly large snail, with a heavy, somewhat swollen, dark brown to black shell, eroded to pearly grey at the top; the shell is plugged by a hemispherical, green and white, calcareous plug or operculum (the cat's eye). Young shells are low, not so heavy, and have prominent ridges which follow the whorls. *Lunella smaragda* lives in pools or on damp flat rock about the middle of the shore. The greatest numbers of this snail occur in the *Corallina* zone on semi-exposed and sheltered shores. Here it is the dominant grazing mollusc, prevailing over *Melagraphia* in competition for food and greatly reducing the growth of seaweed in the zone.

Sypharochiton and all of the snails mentioned are browsers, cropping or scraping up the plant life and detritus. The snails are seemingly indiscriminate as to what they eat, taking in all kinds of minute plants, the early stages of seaweeds and detritus; *Sypharochiton* appears to be selective, showing a preference for the little red seaweed *Gelidium caulacantheum*. *Lunella smaragda* also crops the calcareous seaweed *Corallina officinalis*. Grazing plays an important role in determining whether barnacles or seaweeds are dominant on the broad middle part of the shore: barnacles dominate when the grazers are abundant (unless the seaweeds are already too large for them to eat) and the seaweeds when they are rare or absent. Barnacles keep out the seaweeds by eating their

35

20. *Melagraphia aethiops*, the black top shell. Frequent on reefs sheltered from heavy waves, it is very rarely dominant, mainly due to the strong competition from other grazing snails, the black nerite (*Nerita melanotragus*) from above and the cat's eye (*Lunella smaragda*) from below. Height (of the shell) up to 25 mm.

spores and seaweeds dispose of the barnacles by smothering them or brushing them off the rock. Of course, grazing has little or no effect on this balance between seaweeds and barnacles where other components of the environment such as waves or slope have a great influence on these two kinds of organism.

Finally, three carnivorous snails, *Lepsiella scobina*, the oyster borer, *Neothais scalaris*, the white rock shell, and *Haustrum haustorium*, the dark rock shell. The oyster borer (Figure 22) is fairly small: its shell knobbly, dark brown and fawn, the aperture flecked with white at the edge, and the operculum oval and reddish brown; the body is grey blotched evenly with opaque white. It feeds either by drilling a hole with its tongue through the shell of an oyster or small mussel, or by forcing apart the plates which close off the barnacle from the outside world. Having gained entry, it feeds slowly on the soft insides. *Lepsiella* continues to feed at low tide so long as the shore is still damp. If it is feeding on barnacles, it shows, as might be expected, a distinct preference for large ones (a full stomach for minimum effort); the largest barnacles, however, remain uneaten since the oyster borer cannot penetrate them. When food is abundant the oyster borers grow large and lead separate lives. At times or scarcity, *Lepsiella* forms large groups (usually composed of small individuals) which move over the surface of the rock as a pack systematically attacking the few prey available. *Neothais scalaris* (Figure 23) is a large snail which lives on the lower half of the shore; the shell is heavy and ivory in colour and the operculum is curved, thick and reddish brown. The lower part of the body and the tip of the breathing tube (siphon) are reddish brown, the rest is white. This snail feeds on mussels, gaining entry at a point where the valves do not fit exactly or by wedging the valves apart with the lip of its own shell and then tearing at the soft

36

parts with its tongue. *Neothais scalaris* is particularly common amongst the mussels and barnacles of the exposed coast; it retreats, when the tide ebbs, to the safety of a crevice, depression or gap in the mussel band, and returns to feed with the the advancing tide. *Haustrum* (Figure 24) has a shell which is not as large or as solid as that of *Neothais*; it is dark brown, finely lined with grey, with dark brown also inside the outer lip. The animal is cream with evenly spaces patches of opaque white; the operculum is dark reddish brown. This rock shell prefers mobile shellfish as food, regularly attacking *Lunella, Melagraphia, Nerita* and *Cellana radians*. Access to the soft parts of the prey is won either by boring through the shell (this is the technique used by young rock shells) or smothering the prey first and then inserting the proboscis around the operculum (under the rim of the shell in the case of the limpet).

Predation, like grazing, has a strong influence on the pattern of life of a shore. *Lepsiella* and *Neothais* play a considerable part in determining the lower limit of the barnacles *Chamaesipho brunnea* and *Elminius plicatus*. These predacious snails prey heavily on the barnacles living low down on the shore since at that level they can be active for long periods. Also, by killing single individuals or groups within a pure zone of a particular sedentary species the zone is opened to colonization by other species which, at that time, are producing the young which can occupy the vacant space.

Animals permanently attached to the rock can only close up their openings to the outside world and hope that the thick shell, the 'door' (operculum) or the receding tide or some chance happening prevents the predator from gaining entry; mobile forms, however, can take evasive action. Top shells and limpets, just as soon as they smell (touch is not necessary) a potential predator such as *Haustrum haustorium*, crawl away

21. *Lunella smaragda*, the cat's eye. One of the best-known inhabitants of New Zealand shores; it is especially common on the coralline turf of platform reefs moderately sheltered from waves. When numerous, this herbivorous snail controls the colonization of its zone by other organisms. Height (of the shell) up to 7 cm.

rapidly in the opposite direction. A top shell may be so excited as to raise its shell and swing it through an arc of 180°; this swinging action is often violent enough to shake off a predator trying to grip the prey animal. Some animals, such as *Sypharochiton* and *Nerita*, do not show an escape response.

Some of the mobile animals living on open rock e.g. periwinkles and limpets, obviously do not start off very resistant to the effects of the sun and wind for their delicate young settle and spend the early part of their lives in rock pools, later moving out to the rock face. Other mobile animals probably do the same.

22. *Lepsiella scobina*, the oyster borer: the scourge of rock oysters and barnacles. Numbers of *Lepsiella* are small on shores subject to heavy waves; on the other hand, they are great in quiet waters, for this snail, unlike other rock shells, is very tolerant of silt and cloudy water. The shell of the oyster borer is very variable; the shoulders of the whorls may be quite inconspicuous and the spiral ribs absent. Height (of the shell) up to 27 mm.

Hiding Places or Special Habitats

INTRODUCTION

Although we have had a good look at the animals and plants living in the open, we have really only just started to acquaint ourselves with the large wealth of life on a rocky shore. Most of the inhabitants lie hidden away and we have to get down on our haunches or knees and poke about in all sorts of secret places to find them. The creatures we are looking for cannot survive exposure to the sun and wind and they must therefore remain in damp places when the tide is out. Each of these places offers a special set of living conditions and, as a consequence, harbours a different collection of organisms. Since these places or habitats are so distinct we will consider each one separately.

ON AND UNDER SEAWEEDS

Go to the edge of the sea when the tide is out and pull off a plant of the flapjack (*Carpophyllum maschalocarpum*) or kelp (*Ecklonia radiata*) and swirl it around vigorously in a large, shallow, white tray filled with sea-water. Lots of interesting animals will drop off the seaweed. Many of them will be unknown to you, though perhaps you will recognize some as being related to the common animals of open rock. Do not discard the seaweed yet, for if you look closely at the frond you will see a number of strange growths attached to it. More animals, but of a kind which live permanently fixed to the seaweed. Also attached to the frond are some tiny seaweeds, which could be mistaken for colonial animals. Take a handful of any other seaweed lying on the rock and do the same thing: yet more animals and many of a different sort from those already collected. When the tide retreats a clump of seaweed offers a comfortable refuge from the sun and wind, for it remains moist and cool and also acts as a divided curtain reducing the force of the waves. Naturally, those seaweeds high on the shore do not harbour as rich a collection of animals as those low down. Plants higher up the shore have a longer time to dry out than those at a lower level. The largest clumps offer the most favourable retreat for the cover is dense and the water held within is high; even quite large animals such as crabs and fish find adequate protection here.

Large brown seaweeds offer the most substantial support for fixed species. On *Carpophyllum* or *Ecklonia* you will find colonies of several small, plant-like animals called hydroids or sea-firs. Each hydroid colony consists of a series of runners, often branched, with upright shoots given off at regular intervals. This upright portion may just bear a terminal head or person with a mouth and a circlet of long delicate tentacles or two rows of heads running from the bottom to the top. The delicate flesh or living part of the colony is supported and protected by a horny coat which, in one of the two hydroid groups is also fashioned into a cup around each person. This little 'flower' looks harmless enough, but here appearance is very misleading, for it is a deadly killer of little animals which float or swim in the surrounding water. Whenever a tiny animal brushes against a tentacle, barbed threads

---

CAPTION FOR FIG. 3 (OVERLEAF)

3. Neat zones of animals and plants on a man-made rocky shore, a breakwater (a 30° slope, composed of large rocks bound together by cement mixed with gravel) facing North in a harbour on the East coast of the North Island and subject to moderate waves in stormy weather. EHWS — EXTREME HIGH WATER SPRINGS, ELWS — EXTREME LOW WATER SPRINGS. Extreme tidal range — 3·7m (12 feet).

1. *Porphyra columbina*, a red seaweed, rather like tissuepaper in appearance, which is locally called the karengo; it flourishes in the winter and spring. 1a, a small plant with the frond neatly folded to form a rosette. Up to 20 cm. in diameter.
2. *Littorina unifasciata*, the blue-banded periwinkle, which, at low tide, shelters singly or in groups in crannies and depressions (particularly in the cement). 2a, a side view of an animal extended and crawling. Height of shell up to 12 mm.
3. *Chamaesipho columna*, a small barnacle which has the body plates fused together; occurs in groups (patches in the shorescape) mainly on the steeper facets of the rocks and on the cement. 3a, a group of five individuals. Rarely larger than 5 mm. across.
4. *Crassostrea glomerata*, the rock oyster. 4a, a view of the top (really the right side) of a single individual. Greatest dimension 10 cm.
5. *Gelidium caulacantheum*, a small, bristly, red seaweed giving the rocks a rather patchy knap. 5a, a 'runner' with several upright branches. Height up to 3 cm.
6. *Corallina officinalis*, a jointed, calcareous, red seaweed which forms a fairly even, gritty carpet across the rocks. 6a, a single upright branch. Height up to 8 cm.
7. *Codium adhaerens*, a green seaweed which has the form of lumpy, cushion-like masses, velvety in texture (see figure 5). Greatest dimension up to 20 cm.
8. *Carpophyllum maschalocarpum*, the flapjack and *Ecklonia radiata*, a kelp (see figure 5 for a picture of this seaweed). 8a, a small section of a plant (length up to 1·5 m.) of *Carpophyllum* showing the stem, side branches, 'leaves' and bladders.

40

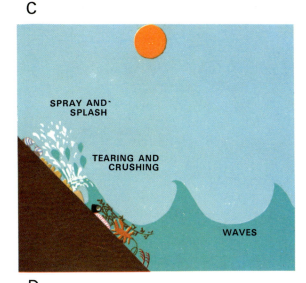

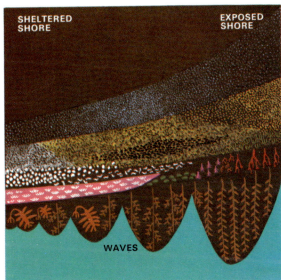

4. The rocky shore environment, much simplified. A and B, the effects of the tide.

A. At low tide (on a sunny day) the rock and organisms are dried and warmed by the wind and sun — the animals are inactive.

B. At high tide the wind and heat of the sun are shut out by the sea and the light is dimmed and altered in composition — the animals are active.

C and D, the waves.

C. Wave action — great pounding and tearing forces are created when a breaking wave curls over to enclose and compress a volume of air and then explodes sending swash and spray up the shore.

D. The effects of the waves. A gradual rise in height (spray from the wave moistens the rock at higher levels making it inhabitable) and change in composition (organisms show different tolerances to waves) of the zones occurs as one follows the rocky shoreline from calm (harbour) to rough (open coast) waters.

1a

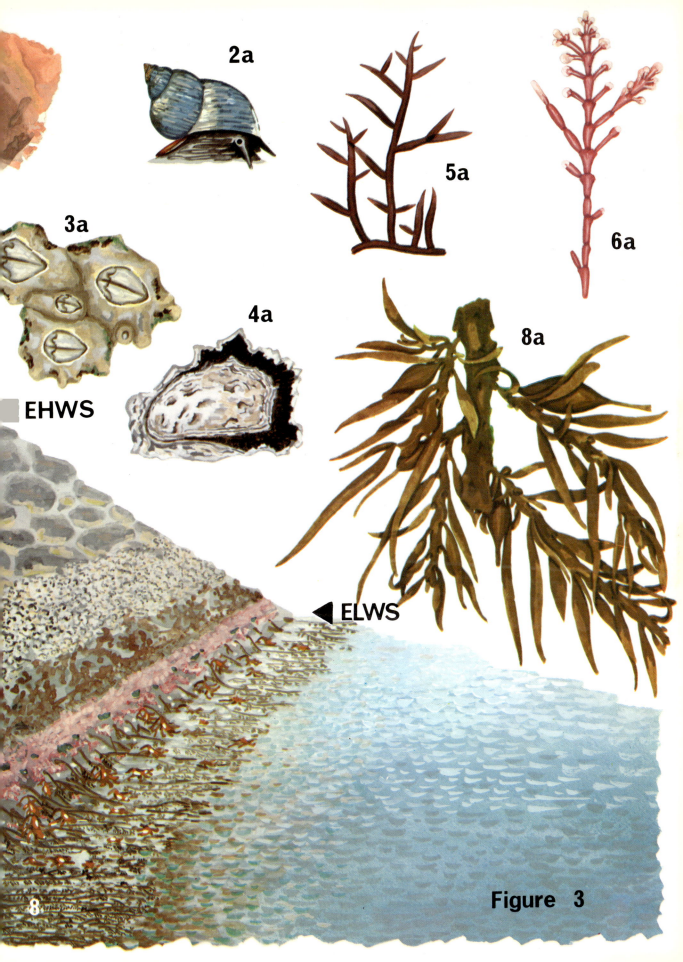

2a

3a

5a

6a

4a

8a

EHWS

◀ ELWS

8

Figure 3

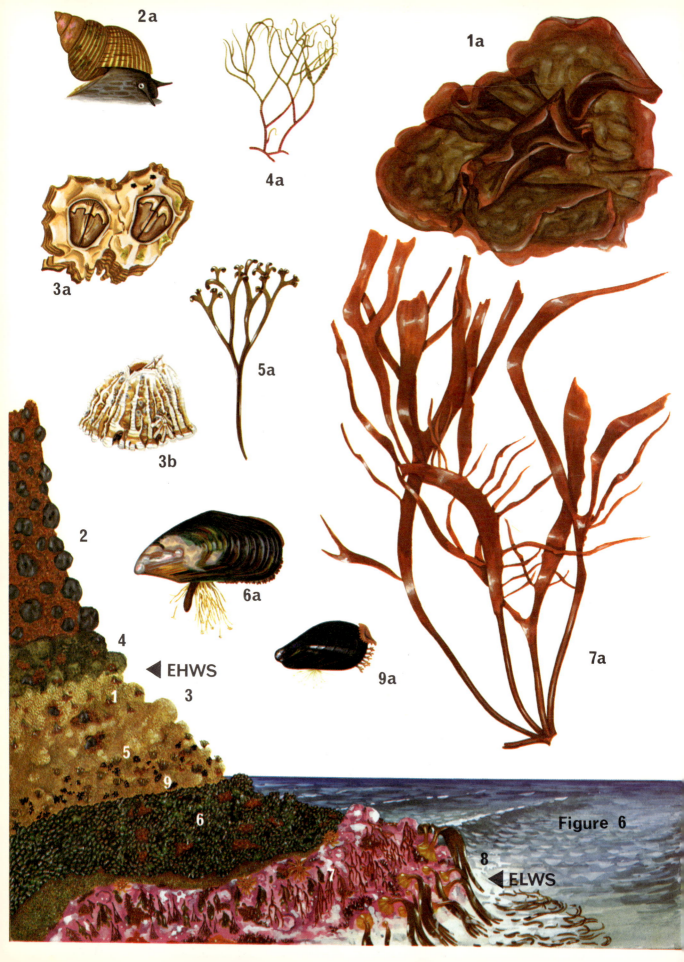

2a

4a

1a

3a

5a

3b

2

7a

4

6a

EHWS

1

3

9a

5

9

Figure 6

6

8

7

ELWS

(nematocysts) are shot out to penetrate, paralyse and hold it. There are many different kinds of hydroid, but we have space to mention only four. *Amphisbetia minima* is one of the double row type, the individuals of the two rows lie opposite to each other. In *Obelia longissima* (Figure 25) there are also two rows of heads, but in this species they are arranged

---

6. Zonation on a shore of breccia (large, broken fragments embedded in larva) facing W. on the West coast of the North Island and continually pounded by heavy waves. As in figure 5 the pattern of zones is very uneven and broken due to the irregular nature of the rock (and consequently the microclimate). EHWS — EXTREME HIGH WATER SPRINGS, ELWS — EXTREME LOW WATER SPRINGS. Extreme tidal range — 3·91 m (12·7 feet).

1. *Porphyra columbina*, the karengo: on this shore the plants grow to a larger size than on the breakwater (see figure 3). 1a, a single, large plant, with much folded frond.
2. *Littorina unifasciata*, the blue-banded periwinkle (see figure 3) and *L. cincta*, the brown-lined periwinkle: both of these snails extend up the shore well beyond the high tide mark, *L. unifasciata* much higher than *L. cincta*. 2a, *L. cincta*, side view of an animal extended and crawling (height of shell up to 19 mm., but usually smaller).
3. *Chamaesipho columna* (see figure 3) *C. brunnea* and *Elminius plicatus*, barnacles: *C. brunnea* dominates the upper part of this zone. 3a, two specimens of *C. brunnea* (rarely larger than 10 mm across). *C. brunnea* occurs in the North Island and the northern half of the South Island. 3b, a specimen of *Elminius plicatus*, a large barnacle commonly occurring in small groups on prominent surfaces of the middle shore in places where there is moderate to heavy wave action (living on this specimen are many *Chamaesipho columna*, one young *E. plicatus*, several young *Modiolus neozelanicus* and *Littorina unifasciata*). Width up to 24 mm.
4. *Bostrychia arbuscula*, a red seaweed: the fronds of fine, branched threads intermingle to form a fairly closely woven carpet. 4a, some upright branches of the frond. Height up to 1 cm.
5. *Gigartina alveata*, a tough red seaweed recognized by the grooved, branched fronds with curled tips: northern half of the North Island only. 5a, a single branch. Height of frond up to 10 cm.
6. *Perna canaliculus*, the green and black mussel. 6a, an individual with the foot (the 'mooring lines' or byssus attached at the base) and cloak (mantle) extended between the valves of the shell. Length up to 17 cm. in shallow water specimens, much smaller on the shore.
7. Red seaweeds (*Pachymenia himantophora*, *Gigartina circumcincta* and *Melanthalia abscissa*) and *Stichaster australis*, the reef star (see figure 7). 7a, a single plant of *Pachymenia himantophora*. Length up to 35 cm. Restricted to the northern 'finger' of the North Island.
8. *Durvillea antarctica*, the bull kelp, forms a dense belt on the lower shore in exposed places (only on wave-battered outlying points on most of the East coast of the North Island). Length up to 10 m.
9. *Modiolus neozelanicus*, the little black mussel which often forms a continuous belt on the middle shore. 9b, a single individual with the byssus and siphons showing. Length up to 19 mm.

alternately and jut out on the ends of short, flexible side-branches. *Orthopyxis crenata* has short upright stems with a single cup at the tip – it looks rather like a tulip flower. On an *Ecklonia* frond you may on occasion find a small jellyfish fixed, right way up i.e. mouth downwards, by special pads on the tentacles. It can detach itself any time and swim to another site. This jellyfish (Figure 26) is the freeswimming stage of the hydroid *Staurocladia hodgsoni* (hydroids normally have a jellyfish stage in their life-history); it is not closely related to the more substantial 'true' jellyfishes of the open sea. The jellyfish stage of *Staurocladia* feeds like the little heads of the hydroid colony. *Staurocladia* has an insignificant permanently attached stage (the stage which draws the common name sea-fir); the tiny feeding heads or polyps, smaller than the jellyfish stage (the medusa), arise singly and at regular but widely spaced intervals along the runners. Being one of the naked type of hydroid, the fleshy head or polyp is not protected by a horny cup and there are two sets of tentacles, the set of these nearest the mouth is knobbed. The jellyfish stage bears the sex cells. Living attached to the brown seaweeds *Cystophora scalaris*, in the south, and *Carpophyllum* is the little sea anemone *Cricophorus nutrix* (Figure 26): though much larger and more solidly built, it is related to the hydroids. Like its relatives, *Cricophorus* is carnivorous, fishing for prey with the tentacles armed with batteries of stinging cells. The body is yellow or brown, sometimes with a greenish or bluish tinge, the top or disc (the mouth lies in the centre) is brown or olive green, and the short tentacles, arranged in several rows along the rim, are light brown. This sea-anemone nurses its young, protecting them within a fold which runs around the body near the base. The sea-mats or polyzoans are common colonial animals. To the untutored these look not unlike the hydroids, for each person has a crown of simple tentacles and lives inside a little horny box. But they are not related. The individuals of the colony are not intimately linked and have a much more complex internal structure. Also, they feed on minute plants which are drawn out of the surrounding water by currents created by the beating of little hair-like processes (cilia) on the tentacles. *Hippothoa bougainvillei* (Figure 27) forms silvery circular patches on the frond of *Ecklonia*.

What of the mobile animals? Commonest are the snails, crabs and shrimp-like creatures of various kinds. There are several kinds of top shell snails (shaped like a child's top), some very beautifully coloured, both the shell and body. *Thoristella oppressa* (Figure 28), a very tiny species, has a shell with a low spire and markedly stepped and finely

42

ridged whorls, fawn or dark brown with some dashes of white. The body of this snail is black and the head and side tentacles grey. *Micrelenchus dilatatus* is a bit bigger with a taller spire and rounded whorls (Figure 29); it is finely lined with light to dark brown on a pink ground, the upper whorls with adjoining dashes of red and white; it is iridescent, particularly around the aperture. The body is light to mid brown and the tentacles are pale yellow. A larger, fairly common top shell is *Trochus viridis* (Figure 30). The shell of this species is an almost perfect top, there being no depressions or swellings between or on the whorls; it is slightly knobbed. The shell is dark violet or purplish brown streaked with dark green; the base is white lined dark purple. The body is yellowish brown overlaid with purple and the frilly skirt, so characteristic of top shells, is opaque white with patches of yellowish brown; the tentacles are purple. *Cantharidus purpuratus* (Figure 31) is another largish top shell, but is not as common as the last. The shell is a tallish cone and is pinkish purple with some brown in places. The body is warty; the ground colour is pale yellow and the depressions between the warts are marked with purple, forming a network pattern. The tentacles are purple. Of these top shells, *Canthari-della tesselata* (Figure 32) is perhaps the prettiest and most variable in colour and pattern. A small snail with a low, swollen shell; it is smooth and glossy, green, fawn, brown, red or violet broken by narrow, irregular strips of white or with regularly spaced, long dashes of white (usually along the widest part of the shell and around the umbilicus) and shorter ones of colour following the coils (contiguous dashes form a distinct pattern of curves). The body is black marked with small, irregular patches of dull yellow. All of these snails feed by scraping up little plants and debris which settle on the surface of the seaweed. Some of them may actually devour the outer tissues of the seaweed.

Shrimp-like animals are common and very varied. *Hippolyte bifidiro-stris* (Figure 33), a local chameleon prawn, is easily recognized by its typically shrimp shaped body which is humped and by the very short, nipper bearing, front limbs: it is usually brown or green. Chameleon prawns are expert at camouflage, imitating the colour and pattern of the background very accurately, though it takes a little time to do so, perhaps a day or so, particularly when adult. A very nimble and quick animal – it darts about from frond to frond with such speed that it is hard to apprehend even when the seaweed is laid out on dry land. Like most prawns, *Hippolyte* is a scavenger, feeding on the decaying remains of small animals and fragments of plants.

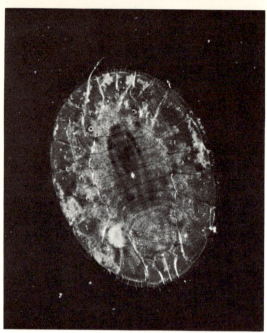

35. *Plakarthrium typicum*, an isopod. Segments one and two of the first feelers and three and four of the second feelers are enlarged to form plates; these plates, along with enlarged trunk and tail plates give the body a perfect elliptical outline. As in *Amphoroidea*, this little isopod grips the kelp tightly; its hold is secured by the powerful hooked claws at the tips of the legs, hooked bristles on the basal joint of the last legs, and projections on the basal joints of the legs and under surface of the head. Length up to 5 mm.

Most of the other shrimp-like animals that inhabit seaweed are either amphipods (sandhoppers and their kin) or isopods (woodlice, sea-slaters and relatives). Although anyone should be able to distinguish between these two groups, it is an expert's job to identify the different kinds, and there are a great many. We can but describe the principal features of the two groups and mention several common and easily identifiable members. The isopods have a flattened body and all the appendages bar the feelers are hidden below. The legs are all much the same in size and shape, except for the rear ones which are plate-like and used for breathing. The female has a brood pouch for nursing the young. Isopods are scavenging or carnivorous in habit, though some do eat living seaweed. A common species living on *Ecklonia* is *Amphoroidea falcifer* (Figure 34), easily distinguished by its axe-shaped head which is separated from the oval body by a narrow 'neck'. Quite large groups are to be found slowly wandering over the surface, feeding on the thick layer of mucilage and the outer cells of the frond. *Amphoroidea* clings so tenaciously to the weed that it needs a strong pull to dislodge it. *Amphoroidea* is beautifully camouflaged, being exactly the colour of its background. Another, much smaller, isopod living on the same brown seaweed is *Plakarthrium typicum* (Figure 35). It is very flat, elliptical in outline, and transparent and colourless except for a few small, opaque yellow spots. This isopod grips the surface of the frond just as tightly as *Amphoroidea*. The other group, the amphipods, are distinguished by the arched, sideways compressed body beset with several different sets of limbs. They swim on their side and can curl the body. Amphipods graze upon very small delicate seaweeds or their microscopic relatives, or on detritus which settles on the surface of

44

seaweeds. A common and very striking species is *Tetradeion crassum*, deep bodied and black, which lives amongst red seaweeds low down on the shore.

Some seaweeds have a large and elaborate 'root' system (the holdfast) and this provides yet another living place for shore animals. Examine the holdfast of an *Ecklonia* plant and you will find the spaces between the branched processes (haptera) packed with all sorts of sponges, worms, shellfish, crustaceans and sea-squirts. Quite a number of the inhabitants live elsewhere on the shore; of these, the bristle worms *Lepidonotus polychroma, Typosyllis brachycola, Odontosyllis polycera, Marphysa depressa* and *Terebella haplochaeta*, the nesting mussel *Ryenella impacta*, and the sea-squirt *Corella eumyota* are described in the sections dealing with crevices, tunnels and loose rocks. We feel that the others are too small and difficult to identify to be considered in this book.

Amongst the larger seaweeds still floating or only partly stranded at the bottom of the shore, in moderately sheltered places, you will find several large, easily recognizable animals. The wandering sea anemone, *Phlyctenactis tuberculosa* (Figure 36), has a flabby, cylindrical body, brownish orange in colour, evenly and closely covered with orange warts; the mouth, at one end, is encircled by short, deep orange tentacles. We do not know how this sea anemone floats. Possibly like many floating forms, it is due to the animal having in its body less of the heavy chemicals and more of the lighter ones than the surrounding sea water; this difference in quantity being controlled by internal processes. Buoyancy may be the result of the secretion of gas in the tissues. Like other sea anemones, *Phlyctenactis* is a carnivore catching living prey with stinging cells the same as those of its other relatives, the hydroids and jellyfish.

Notomithrax ursus (Figure 37), the hairy seaweed crab, stands or moves quietly beneath the seaweed canopy. Usually it is perfectly camouflaged by the small seaweeds attached to the special hooked hairs on its back and legs. The crab fastens the seaweeds to itself with the pincers which are mobile and can reach all of the hooked hairs. Before fixing a plant, the point of attachment is chewed by the crab, possibly to coat it with a glue-like secretion. When *Notomithrax* is not dressing itself in weed or feeding, the pincers are held neatly folded under the body. If you turn this crab over, you will see that the parts not obscured by the hairs are pleasantly coloured; the pincers are henna except for the fingers which are white touched with greyish blue, the legs are also greyish blue, so is the under surface of the body but here the colour is relieved with large, regularly spaced, areas of white.

45

Small individuals of Cook's turban, *Cookia sulcata*, graze the fronds of the flapjack and kelp. A full-grown *Cookia* (Figure 38) is a large snail and when it becomes too heavy to be supported by the seaweed it moves to the rock to scrape the encrusting calcareous seaweed for food. Occasionally, specimens will be found uncovered by the tide, often wedged in large fissures in the rock. A close relative of the much commoner cat's eye; the heavy plug or operculum is the most obvious mark of their affinity, though in *Cookia* it is almost oval and unevenly calcified. The shell, a low cone, is very rough: it is ribbed and finely ridged, some of the ridges being raised to form a tile-like pattern where they cross the ribs. Though sometimes capped with purplish pink calcareous seaweed, the shell is usually fawn and green, streaked with black; in young snails there is a thin, brown, fibrous coat, but in older ones this has usually been worn away. The soft body is dark yellowish green, lighter and more yellow higher up; the head is grey, striped horizontally with dark brown. As in the cat's eye, there is a single pair of body tentacles.

In fairly quiet, clear water you will sometimes be lucky enough to find the local sea-horse, *Hippocampus abdominalis* (Figure 39). You would probably see it more often if it did not blend in so well with its habitat: depending on the predominant colour of the local seaweed it may be brown, purplish grey, green or red, sometimes mottled with patches of a brighter tint. Camouflage is the sea-horse's main defence since the thin, bony plates of the body offer only limited protection. It moves between the fronds of the seaweed with such grace, quiet dignity and precision that one may wonder whether the driving and guiding forces are supernatural, but the animal is fully responsible for its movements, propelling itself by waving the fin of the back and the tiny fins at the sides of the head. When a sea-horse is feeding or resting, or the water movement is strong, it hangs on to the seaweed with its highly flexible tail (here the bony plates are ring-like and jointed), coiling the tip around the support just as a spider monkey would do when swinging through the trees. The sea-horse feeds on small crustaceans such as the amphipods and isopods described earlier in this chapter. The tubular muzzle is poked here and there amongst the vegetation, and when prey is sighted the tiny mouth is placed close to it, opened and the unfortunate crustacean sucked in (in the respiratory current). Strangely enough, it is the male which cares for the young: he has a large pouch which gives him a pot-bellied appearance, especially when it is swollen with the developing offspring. The eggs, 200 or so,

46

are placed in the brood pouch by the female (sometimes several females in turn); she connects her genital opening with the aperture of the pouch and forces the eggs in (this is the moment when they are fertilized). Birth seems quite an exhausting business: the male, gripping the seaweed, holds himself rigid and contracts the pouch powerfully, expelling the young animals which are now miniatures of the adult.

ROCK POOLS

A rock pool would seem to offer shore organisms a refuge from the rigours of the open rock climate and a way by which they could extend up the shore to a level higher than that reached on open rock. This is not quite so. Changes in the living conditions within pools are often much greater and more sudden than on open rock. Also, not all of the characteristic inhabitants of open rock can live in pools for many of them have become so adapted to regular exposure to the air that they dislike being permanently submerged.

Whether or not an organism raises its level on the shore by living in a pool, or even that it lives in a pool at all, depends on what happens to the pool water during the ebb tide. A body of water isolated by the tide changes in quality: during the day it becomes either more or less salty, due to evaporation or rain respectively, hot or cold, depending on the air temperature, saturated with oxygen and depleted in carbon dioxide due to the activity of the seaweeds and thus becomes alkaline. The tide floods and the conditions in the pool quickly revert to those of the open sea. Ebb tide at night also produces changes, though these are mainly opposite those which take place during the day: oxygen is now low and carbon dioxide high, for the seaweeds, like all green plants, cannot photosynthesize (photosynthesis is the manufacture of energy-rich substances using carbon dioxide and water and releasing oxygen as a by-product) without light, and the water becomes acidic. The extent of these changes mainly depends on two things; the size and the position of the pool. The changes are only slight in a large pool near low water and very great in a small pool or pan at high water or just above. But it is not just vertical position or size which control the habitability of a rock pool. Shape is extremely important. The perfect pool is a basin with uniform living conditions or, if they vary at all, then the variation from one part to another is very slight and gradual. Few pools are like this; they are usually irregular with miniature canyons and

47

ridges, ledges, crevices, precipices and plains, and the living conditions are equally varied. It may be the steepness of the slope or the intensity of the light which determines where certain organisms can live. It may be the quality of the water: during the time a pool is separated from the sea only the surface layers of water may be altered in quality and consequently organisms living at the bottom will not be subjected to this change. It may be the amount of firm surface at a given part of the pool and a crevice provides plenty; many animals only feel secure when they have a high degree of contact with the bottom. The conditions in the pool will also be altered by the weather, fresh water as rain or seepage from the land, shade and the activities of the inhabitants, whether it is the photosynthesis of the seaweeds, the respiration and excretion of animals or the decomposition of dead organisms by bacteria. The distribution of plants and animals in a pool is governed by one of these conditions or by several acting together. Every pool you examine shows a different pattern of life, the reason being that no two pools are exactly alike in position, size, shape and how they are affected by the local climate. Even with such variety, a quick look over the shore will tell you that there is a gradient in the richness of pool life, being

8. Seaweeds.

1, a blue-green; 2–5, greens; 6–9, browns.

1. *Calothrix scopulorum*, a characteristic high level species of gently sloping, muddy sandstone shores. Length of threads up to 1 mm.
2. *Ulva lactuca*, the sea lettuce, luxuriant in summer, particularly on the middle shore of the open coast. Length up to 45 cm.
3. *Enteromorpha intestinalis*, a summer species particularly abundant in brackish pools high on the shore. Length up to 30 cm.
4. *Enteromorpha compressa*, lives at a high level and is abundant where there is fresh water seepage. Length up to 15 cm.
5. *Chaetomorpha linum*, profuse in summer in high level pools, particularly on the open coast. Length up to 20 cm.
6. *Bachelotia fulvescens*, often abundant though local in occurrence in high level pools of the upper shore and also on some large seaweeds (such as *Hormosira banksii*). Length up to 5 cm.
7. *Glossophora kunthii*, an open coast species, most plentiful in winter; lives at a low level on rock (forms a zone in some places) and in rock pools (plants are smaller). Length up to 45 cm.
8. *Zonaria angustata,* another lower shore species of the open coast though not as common as the previous one, lives on rock and in tide pools: the plants vary considerably in shape and size with habitat. Length up to 35 cm., but usually shorter.
9. *Ralfsia verrucosa*, occurs, often abundantly, on rock and shells on moderately sheltered to exposed shores. Greatest dimension up to 12 cm.

Figure 8

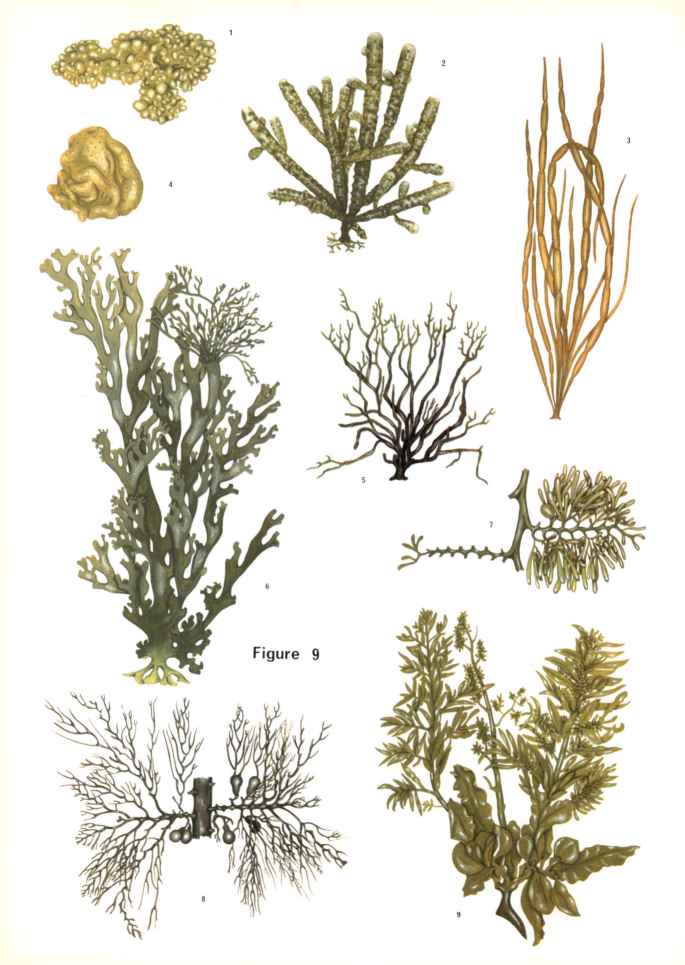

Figure 9

luxuriant at low water and sparse at high water (this is most noticeable if the pools being compared decrease in size towards the top of the shore). Unfortunately we have not the space to describe the complete range of pools. To demonstrate this great variation we will take a look at two pools, a large deep one at low tide and a small, shallow one near high water.

A large pool abounds in life (Figure 40). The vegetation is luxuriant: the brown seaweeds are often so profuse as to form a thick carpet across the surface of the water. A common brown in pools on fairly quiet shores is *Carpophyllum plumosum* (Figure 9.8), a close relative of the flapjack; it is olive brown and has a long flat stem and evenly and finely divided side branches, held at the surface by little, stalked, gas-filled, bladders. It is very fluffy in appearance and it reminds one of the feather boa worn by Edwardian ladies. Another bulky brown is *Cystophora torulosa* (Figure 9.7), characteristic of pools on the open coast. It is a fleshy olive brown plant: the stem is thick and zigzags sharply, and the narrower side branches bear clusters of club-shaped leaflets, supported by globular floats. *Sargassum sinclairi* (Figure 9.9), another common

---

9. Seaweeds, all browns.

1. *Leathesia difformis*, often very common growing on rocks and other seaweeds at a low level on the shore; it is dominant in spring and summer. Greatest dimension up to 10 cm.

2. *Splachnidium rugosum*, the gummy weed, grows on rock on the middle shore (spring to autumn in the north, all the year round in the south); dominant in summer and autumn. Length up to 20 cm.

3. *Scytosiphon lomentaria*, a species of the middle shore, occurring on rock and in pools, most common in winter and spring. Length up to 25 cm.

4. *Colpomenia sinuosa*, occurs, attached to rock or seaweeds (particularly *Corallina officinalis*), at a low level on gently sloping reefs, moderately sheltered; dominant in spring and summer. Diameter up to 18 cm.

5. *Scytothamnus australis*, grows on rock on the middle shore. Length up to 45 cm.

6. *Xiphophora chondrophylla*, a low level species, grows on rock or in pools along the open coast where the sea surges strongly; distribution is rather patchy. Length up to 1 m.

7. *Cystophora torulosa*, a species which lives in large, low level pools and areas of standing water in sheltered places along the open coast. Length up to 80 cm. Only a small section of the frond is shown.

8. *Carpophyllum plumosum*, as the previous species but penetrates into harbours; restricted to the eastern side of the North Island. Length up to 1 m. Only a small section of the frond is shown.

9. *Sargassum sinclairii*, often present in low level rock pools and channels on all shores except the most wave-beaten. Length up to 60 cm.

pool-dwelling brown, is a close relative of the famous drifting seaweed which gives its name to that area of calm water in the Central Atlantic, known as the Sargasso Sea. The local *Sargassum* is olive to yellow in colour and has a smooth, circular holdfast from which arise short, thick, knotty stems bearing large spear shaped 'leaves'. From this rosette issue long narrow branches carrying 'leaves' which become progressively smaller and narrower towards the tip; at the bases of these 'leaves' are reproductive bodies and ellipsoidal bladders. In pools on open coasts are found two more browns, both easily identifiable – *Glossophora kunthii*, which we have already described from open rock, and *Zonaria angustata* (Figure 8.8). *Zonaria* is papery to the touch, irregularly branched with fan-like tips, dark olive brown grading to yellowish green apically and marked with narrow curved bands (reproductive bodies). It is very variable in form; it can be compact (pools low on the shore) or very long with narrow widely separated branches (pools at a higher level). Two other browns are very common, Neptune's Necklace (*Hormosira banksii*) growing along the rim and the common kelp, *Ecklonia radiata*, anchored well below the surface of the pool. A low tidal pool is the best place to seek red seaweeds. There are a great many different kinds, but we can only mention a few of them here. *Pterocladia pinnata* (Figure 10.3), a common species, has a frond consisting of a narrow, flat stem with branches arising from the upper part, regularly and squarely. It is rather stiff and tough, and is reddish brown. A very attractive and easily recognizable red is *Champia novaezelandiae* (Figure 10.8). A narrow runner gives off groups of fairly wide and tall 'stems', each usually heavily branched at the tip (looks like a group of fat 'fingers'). *Champia* is a delicate purplish pink with a blue iridescence, marked by regularly spaced dark bars (internal partitions). Large but shallow pools further up the shore are usually carpeted with *Corallina officinalis*, already mentioned earlier, and commonly intermingled with it is *Laurencia thyrsifera* (Figure 10.9). The frond of *Laurencia* is olive green to pinkish red and has a distinct cylindrical main 'stem' and much divided side branches with broadly rounded tips. Neptune's Necklace (*Hormosira banksii*) is often abundant in these same pools (it can extend up to high water mark). The 'beads' of a pool plant are fairly large and are connected by rather long links.

So many animals live in low tidal pools that it is quite impossible for us to mention more than the most obvious and commonest. Nestling at the edge, especially where there is a depression, fissure or corner, you will find groups of *Evechinus chloroticus*, the common large sea

50

urchin, the sea-egg or kina. Nowadays individuals found on the shore are fairly small for they are so heavily and regularly harvested that there is little chance of an individual reaching a large size. The sea-egg (Figure 41) is covered with strong, fairly long spines, grading towards the tip from metallic blue to green then yellow and finally white. The delicate skin covering the body is deep red. A strong pull is needed to tear a sea-egg from the rock for it ties itself down firmly by its tube feet (there are ten narrow tracts of these). A sea-egg often camouflages itself with pieces of shell and small stones which are held against the body by some of the tube feet. The sea-egg moves by first extending the lowermost tube feet of the rows on the leading side, fixing them to the rock by a terminal pad and then contracting them drawing the body towards the point of fixation. The trailing tube feet are first stretched and then released. The tube feet are assisted by the movable spines (there is a ball and socket joint between the base of the spine and the body) acting as levers. Lift a sea-egg from the pool and turn it upside down. You will see the mouth in the centre of an area clear of spines and if you watch long enough you will observe the animal protrude a hard white cone-like structure, a ring of five, large, triangular teeth (the business end of a structure named Aristotle's lantern). These teeth are thrust out of the mouth and drawn apart at the same time, then withdrawn and together: by moving its teeth in this way the sea-egg scrapes encrusting animals, small seaweeds and debris from the surface of the rock. Like the hedgehog and porcupine, the sea-egg defends itself with its spines; not a very inviting mouthful for a hungry fish, though some do eat them. The body is also protected against little animals which attempt to settle on it. Amongst the bases of the spines are little pincers which are used to hold, nip or crush would-be squatters.

Sea-hares are often encountered in large pools on moderately exposed coasts. These animals are shellfish (of a kind related to the snails) with the shell reduced to a thin plate enclosed in a flap of skin at the top of the plump fleshy body. Like a land snail or slug, there are two pairs of tentacles on the head; a large rolled front pair and a smaller pointed and grooved pair, the 'hare's ears', further back on top of the head. *Aplysia dactylomela* is a big species of sea-hare; it is easily recognized by its olive green body marked with a network and circles of black pigment. The red seaweeds *Corallina officinalis* and *Laurencia* are the favourite food of *Aplysia dactylomela*. Occasionally large herds of these animals are formed during the reproductive season.

Peering down into the pool you will notice that the floor is littered with snails. To your surprise many of these snails move about with a jerkiness and speed unusual for such a slowcoach of an animal. Look closely and you will see that it is not a snail but a hermit crab living inside a snail's shell. There are several kinds of hermit crab living on local shores; the commonest is *Pagurus novaezelandiae*, quickly identified by its blue, hairy walking legs and knobbly pincers (Figure 42). The hermit crab has a soft, flexible and twisted abdomen with a pair of small, strong limbs at the tip, modifications for fitting and gripping the inside of the snail's shell. It can withdraw its body very quickly. As the hermit grows he must of necessity change his size in shells. Each shell he chooses fits fairly snugly, neither too sloppy nor too tight. When the shell starts to pinch a bit the hermit, in his travels about the pool or over the rock when the tide is in, meets and tests empty snail shells for size and quality. If a suitable shell is found, then it is swopped for the old one very quickly; it has to be fast for the naked hermit makes a tasty morsel.

Squat motionless and peer into the rock pool. At times you have the feeling that you are looking at something but cannot make out what it is. A longer, harder look and at last you can see it; it is the prawn *Palaemon affinis* (Figure 43). It is so transparent that it is hardly surprising that you could not see it at first. When you examine the prawn closely you will see that it is not completely transparent; it is lined with brown or black, there is a large black spot ringed with orange on each side at the base of the last limbs (which form the tail fan) and the walking legs are banded with orange and black above the joints. By contracting and expanding the lines of pigment the prawn can lighten or darken its body in response to the background. *Palaemon* can walk sedately on its legs, swim gracefully by flapping the little limbs of the abdomen, or shoot away suddenly by a quick bending of the tail. Both hermit crab and the prawn are scavengers, that is, they are members of the great refuse disposal corps of the shore, removing, by eating, dead and dying animals and pieces of vegetation. The food is cut, handled, and eventually passed to the mouth by the pincer-bearing walking legs and the special feeding limbs.

At the bottom of a deep pool, where there are patches of shell and gravel, lives the large sea-anemone *Isocradactis magna* (Figure 44). When it is open only the disc with central mouth and circle of tentacles is revealed; the body or column remains buried in the shell gravel. This sea-anemone gains added protection by plastering the upper part of the body with pieces of broken shell and small stones and using these to fill the hole left when it contracts. The body is fawn and the tubercles

52

48. *Zeacumantus subcarinatus*, the small horn shell (a cerith), is common in pools and on flat rock which is fairly free of silt and remains damp at low tide. A shorter spire with a slightly curved outline and an aperture with a thickened outer lip and narrow canal distinguish this species from its relative *Zeacumantus lutulentus*. Height of shell up to 15 mm.

49. *Stiliger felinus*, a sea-slug which lives in pools at the boundary of the middle and upper shore zones on the open coast; it is often very abundant during the summer months when there is a heavy growth of its food plant *Chaetomorpha linum*. *Stiliger* is very tolerant of changes in salinity and temperature. When individuals (each is both male and female) copulate, the sperms are injected with a stylet (like a short hypodermic needle) through the body wall, not by way of the female opening: old individuals are usually well-scarred, the 'wounds' of many sexual connexions. Length up to 13 mm.

grey, and the tentacles are blue, mauve, orange or white. There the anemone stands with its tentacles extended, inviting a prawn or small fish to rest upon it. If one is rash enough even to brush against a tentacle, it is quickly paralysed by stinging cells and then gradually pushed into the mouth by the tentacles. The prey is mostly of a large size and this counteracts the infrequency of meals.

Another carnivore is the common cockabully, *Tripterygium robustum* (Figure 45); small prawns and amphipods are its favourite food. Like the prawn, it is shy and nervous and quick to detect movement. One has to remain very still so as not to frighten it into hiding. Adults are black with white markings and the fins along the back, particularly the little front one, are daubed with red. On the head, just above the eye, is a little branched process.

The plant and animal life in a pool at the top of the shore (Figure 46) is much less varied, though some of the species are abundant. Some of the inhabitants are open rock forms which reached this high level by living permanently immersed. Most obvious of these are the seaweeds *Hormosira banksii* and *Corallina officinalis* and the animals *Sypharochiton pelliserpentis*, *Pomatoceros caeruleus*, *Crassostrea glomerata* and *Nerita melanotragus*, all of which have been described before. A high level pool is also the nursery for young periwinkles. You will notice, however, some plants and animals not met with before, all of them able to extend, in pools, higher on the shore than most of those just mentioned. All of these organisms can cope, each in its own special way, with the extreme and fluctuating conditions of such a pool. A small number of seaweeds dominate these pools. Two are greens; *Enteromorpha intestinalis* (Figure 8.3), light in colour, thin, tubular and unbranched, and *Chaetomorpha linum*, dark and threadlike (Figure 8.5). Another seaweed is the brown *Bachelotia fulvescens* which often forms a yellowish brown gelatinous turf; each plant consists of numerous exceedingly fine and sparsely branched filaments. Three animals are common inhabitants of these pools. *Siphonaria zelandica* (Figure 47) is a limpet-like relative of the land snails; it has a thick, fleshy body, just too big for the shell, mottled yellow and black. On the right side, below a small extension of the shell, is a pore protected by thick lips which leads into the 'lung' (unlike the land snails it contains a gill and is filled with water). Another snail is *Zeacumantus subcarinatus* (Figure 48), a cerith (sometimes called creepers). The shell is a tall spire of many whorls, reddish brown to black in colour. The body is grey marked with black and speckled with opaque white and the tentacles are ringed with white. *Zeacumantus* feeds on *Corallina* and fine debris which collects on the floor of the pool. Finally there is the little black sea-slug *Stiliger felinus* (Figure 49), quite naked with the back adorned with club-shaped processes. For all its nakedness it is not defenceless, for there are glands in the skin which produce a nasty tasting white substance and this is released whenever the animal is irritated. This sea-slug feeds on *Chaetomorpha* by slitting the wall of the seaweed with its sharp 'tongue' and sucking out the sap.

OVERHANGS, CREVICES AND TUNNELS

Most rocky shores are uneven, cracked and pitted – the handiwork of the waves and weather, and, to a lesser extent the organisms. Different types of rock are worn away at different speeds, and as a consequence ledges, crevasses, little caves and crevices are formed, all making excellent retreats for shore animals when the tide goes out. Like open rock and rock pools there is a gradation in the living conditions; there is a gradual decrease in habitability for sea organisms as one goes up the shore. Obviously a little cave or crevice at the top of the shore has longer to dry out in than one at the bottom. Aspect is also important for a cave or crevice shielded from the sun and wind does not dry out as rapidly as one facing them. The living conditions offered by an overhang and a crevice do permit organisms to extend up the shore to a level much higher than on open rock. Such hiding places are so varied in shape and position that all we can do here is describe two examples, an overhang near low water and a crevice at the middle of the shore.

Large protected overhangs have a very rich fauna because the surface remains damp at ebb tide. Plant-like animals are abundant here: sponges, hydroids, barnacles, sea-anemones, sea-mats and sea-squirts abound, often so common as to completely cover the surface of the rock (Figure 50). Here is rich and varied colour, only matched on the undersurfaces of loose rocks standing at low tide mark on permanently submerged rock. The sea surges and eddies about these overhangs, keeping the surface moist and bringing fresh supplies of food, both so important to fixed animals. Very obvious members are the golf ball sponge, *Tethya aurantium* (Figure 51), a largish yellowish orange to orange sphere with the surface of the upper hemisphere raised to form little paving stones'; from the smooth lower half issue 'runners' which pass across the rock giving rise to other 'golf balls'. This is just one of many sponges which live on overhangs: another is *Suberites axellinoides*, an encrusting type which is particularly common; it forms smallish, fairly thin, somewhat slimy patches, orange in colour. There are some fairly bulky species: *Ancorina alata* is one of the largest of these; it looks rather like a large lump of kneaded dough, steel grey in colour, but to the touch it is hard and rough; it gives off a sulphurous odour. Sponges feed on very small particles of organic matter and minute organisms such as bacteria which are separated from the current of water drawn through the body of the sponge when it is immersed.

Two sea-anemones are common, both sleek and prettily coloured. *Actinothoe albocincta* has alternating lines of grey white and orange down the body and white tentacles (Figure 52). *Diadumene neozelanica* (Figure 53) has stripes of grey on a colourless ground and orange tentacles. When extended for feeding it is easily distinguished from *Actinothoe* by the two-tiered body. Another sea-anemone, the sea-waratah (*Actinia tenebrosa*), although a common inhabitant of overhangs at a higher level, is too obvious a feature of our shores to be overlooked here. Usually it is seen as a fairly big hemisphere of dark red jelly with a small hole at the top. However, when covered by the sea it opens to feed, showing its claret coloured body with a row of cobalt blue swellings along the upper edge and circles of vivid red tentacles (Figure 54). *Actinia* is a particularly hardy sea anemone, making an excellent tenant for your home sea water aquarium. This sea anemone, like *Cricophorus* which lives on brown seaweeds (see the previous chapter), broods its young, but in this case they are held inside the gut, not in a special pouch. The parent liberates the juveniles by contracting its body and blowing them out of the mouth. Like the other sea-anemones described previously, *Actinia tenebrosa* is a carnivore.

Groups of a very pretty barnacle, *Balanus trigonus*, are common on overhangs in harbour waters; it is wide and flat and the side plates are strongly ribbed and reddish pink with intervening white segments. Like *Chamaesipho* species of the open rock, it catches food by casting a 'net' of bewhiskered legs.

Sea-mats abound, both crust and tree-like kinds; but more about these when we describe the fauna of loose stones and rocks.

Sea squirts are also very common, and are also varied and beautifully coloured. Two solitary species are characteristic of overhangs: *Microcosmus kura* (Figure 55), common in harbours, is tough and irregularly veined, and with tubercles around the base of each siphon, and in colour, grading from the base, fawn, purple and mid brown; *Asterocarpa*

56

coerulea (Figure 56), especially common in the clear waters of the open coast, is much lower and smoother, and is regularly grooved and coloured cream and blue. To the untutored, the solitary sea squirt looks a simple sort of animal; a tough bag with two short tubes (siphons), each with an opening from which squirts a jet of water when the animal is poked or knocked. Inside this bag, however, is a complex animal, a very distant relative of ourselves and other vertebrates. A sea squirt feeds and breathes by drawing in water through one of the openings, the mouth, passing it through a basket-like part of the gut, where food particles and organisms are strained out and respiratory gases exchanged, and finally expelling it through the other aperture, the atrial opening.

A crevice (Figure 57) provides a comfortable home for many sorts of animals. Like the overhang it is dimly lit, damp and cool, but differs in having restricted space and poor water circulation, and in being partly filled with broken shell, small stones and silt. Of course, like the overhang, living conditions will differ according to the size, shape and position on the shore, the nature of the rock and the direction the entrance faces, seaward or landward, north or south. The very narrowness of a crevice affords animals with a living condition not provided by an overhang; in a crevice mobile animals can gain maximum contact with the surface of the rock thus giving them greater security. As a consequence of this some fairly large mobile forms number among the inhabitants of crevices. A crevice can be divided roughly into three zones: (1) the region just inside the opening, fairly dry, bright and cool, and quite free of loose material; (2) a middle region, dim, damp and cool, filled with broken shell, small stones and coarse sand and having moderate circulation of water; (3) an inner region filled with silt and clay, dark and waterlogged, except for some small pockets of air, and having little or no water circulation. The quality and quantity of the sediment lodged inside the crevice will depend on the strength of the water movement at that particular point on the shore. Where the wave action is strong the material in the crevice will be coarse. The crevice community includes both permanent and temporary members – some animals spend the whole of their adult lives within the crevice, others retire there temporarily when the tide ebbs, or only live there permanently whilst young, or occur there accidentally, perhaps thrown in by a wave.

For the sake of simplicity, let us look at a crevice at the middle of the shore. The outer zone is permanently occupied by the barnacle *Chamaesipho columna*, or in quiet waters, by *Elminius modestus. Pomatoceros caeruleus*, the tube worm, also lives here. Where such a crevice holds standing water, the olive green sea anemone, *Isactinia olivacea* (Figure 58), is common. The middle zone is the retreat for two common bristle worms of the crawling kind. *Eulalia microphylla* (Figure 59), a very active and nervous worm, is very long and slender and has a dark green body flanked by tiny pale yellowish green paddle-like processes. On a damp day this worm can often be found feeding on moribund barnacles. The other bristle worm is the rag-worm *Perinereis novaehollandiae* (Figure 60): it is bluish green in colour, dark at the head end and paler towards the tail with a conspicuous red line (a blood vessel) down the middle of the back; although this worm may reach a length of two

65. A close-up of a vertical face of soft rock (mudstone) which has been heavily bored by animals, mainly piddocks. Many of the original tunnellers are dead (though their shells are still present in various states of decay) and their homes are occupied by such animals as sea-anemones, bristle worms, snails and crabs.

66. *Anchomasa similis*, the large rock borer or piddock: this bivalve shellfish drills a burrow, head end usually downwards, in mudstone or sandstone reefs below mid tidal level; spoil is flushed from the burrow with a jet of water from around the foot which is produced by a sharp closure of the shell. A tiny bivalve, *Arthritica crassiformis*, cohabits with *Anchomasa*, groups of two or three individuals, occurring along the edge of the piddock's fleshy mantle. Although *Anchomasa* is found throughout New Zealand, it is uncommon in the south. Length (of the shell) up to 68 mm.

feet and be as thick as the little finger, individuals normally found are considerably smaller. *Perinereis* feeds on live and dead plants and animals; it tears its food with a short, very muscular, tube, the proboscis, armed with jaws and groups of little teeth, and the fragments are then swallowed. Another inhabitant of the middle zone is *Onchidella nigricans* (Figure 61), a short slug-like animal related to the land-snails. From above it is elliptical in outline with a crenate margin: the skin is rubbery and fairly rough, marbled black, grey and brown in differing proportions; underneath it is smooth and pale grey. At the hind end, between the foot and the back, is a conspicuous pore which is the opening of the 'lung'. *Onchidella* is truly amphibious, using its 'lung' to breathe when the tide is out and the moist skin when the tide is in. The small head bears a pair of short, knobbed tentacles. *Onchidella* is very active when the shore is damp and can move about at an incredible pace for a member of the snail group: it feeds on the surface film of minute plants and debris which it rakes up with its hard 'tongue'.

An orange ribbon worm, *Amphiporus* sp. (Figure 62), is a common member of the middle zone group. Like all ribbon worms, it has a deceptive appearance, for though it looks clumsy and slow, and it is

59

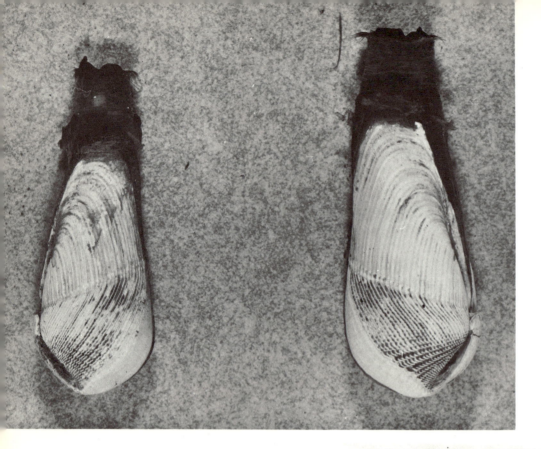

67. *Pholadidea spathulata*, the commonest of the two local paper piddocks, lives side by side with *Anchomasa* though not reaching as high a level on the shore. The tip of the long, fleshy, respiratory-feeding tube (fused siphons) is rather different from that of *Anchomasa*; the two openings are surrounded by a ring of slender tentacles, and the lower one (entrance for the water current) has a ring of tree-like processes which interlock and act as a grating (to exclude large particles) or, if drawn tightly together, as a door. Specimens of the other paper piddock, *Pholadidea tridens*, may, on occasion, be encountered; it is distinguished from *P. spathulata* by a posterior, partly calcareous, tube-like extension of the shell. Length (of the shell) up to 45 mm.

68. *Zelithophaga truncata*, the date mussel, a boring bivalve shellfish which is common in the lower two-thirds of the piddock zone. The animal in the photograph (taken from below) has its shell open, revealing the fleshy mantle, and breathing-respiratory tube or siphon (darkly pigmented) protruded: also visible is the horny coat or periostracum which protects the shell against abrasion and, possibly, acid secreted by the animal. Length (of the shell) up to 36 mm.

when crawling about, it is very quick indeed at mealtimes. *Amphiporus* lassos its prey, usually an annelid worm bigger than itself, in an instant with a long, narrow, sticky, tubular structure, the proboscis (this is kept tucked away in a sheath when not in use): the proboscis is equipped with a sharp tooth, the stylet, which is used to wound the prey and thus bring about the rapid entry of a poison. The ribbon worm, just like the boa constrictor, swallows its prey whole.

The innermost zone of the crevice is only sparsely inhabited: the animals living there are species which make permanent burrows which they have to continually flush to prevent stagnation. Two obvious, large and striking members are bristle worms. *Timarete anchylochaeta* (Figure 63), in shape and colour, is rather like a small, slender cigar festooned with red (gills) and white (feelers) 'ribbons'. The feelers or tentacles are used to convey small particles of detritus to near the head end; there the particles collect in clumps which the worm swallows periodically. The other bristle worm is *Terebella haplochaeta* (Figure 64); the body is long, tapered and red and white in colour with a cluster of long, grooved, colourless tentacles and two pairs of bright red (gorged with blood) tree-like gills at the swollen front end. It is very active animal, ceaselessly sending waves of contraction along its body which drive water through the burrow, and putting out and drawing in its very mobile tentacles. The tentacles are used to collect food, mainly particles of organic matter, and convey it to the head. As the particles reach the head they are wiped off the tentacles by the lips of the mouth; large particles are rejected, small particles are fashioned into a roll and swallowed.

Where the rock is soft mudstone and lies near low water, homes are cut in it by a small number of animals, each specially adapted for boring. They all work with such industry that the outer layers of rock are soon so greatly drilled (Figure 65) as to be very weak and easily broken with a spade, strong knife or hatchet, or naturally by the waves. Largest amongst these tunnellers are the piddocks (there are three species). *Anchomasa similis* (Figure 66) is the biggest piddock; the shell is in two halves, like other bivalve shellfish, but the valves are long, rounded at the rear, and notched and pointed and covered with wavy ridges at the other (the bit of the drill). The smoother part of the shell is covered with a delicate, honey yellow fibrous 'skin', the periostracum, which is worn away in places and here the white shell shows. The shell is sometimes discoloured black. A round plug-like foot, cream in colour, protrudes through the hole formed by the notched lower edges of the shell. On the other side there is a separate, shield-shaped piece of shell. On the lower side the shells cannot be closed and the dirty, pale yellow flesh is visible. At the hind end the body is drawn out into a long, highly contractile, fleshy tube, the tip of which is covered with little pimples set against a violet brown background. At the tip of this tube, which is often protruded from the tunnel, are two openings, the entrance (lower and larger one with a ring of small tentacles) and exit (upper) for the respiratory-feeding current. This tube is very mobile and can be extended to a length about equal to the length of the shell. *Pholadidea spathulata* (Figure 67), one of the other two piddocks, is very similar in design: it differs, however, in the details of the shell. In the adult animal, which has given up drilling, the front end of the shell is bulbous and complete with the lower part smooth; there is no permanent gap between the valves for the foot to protrude through. Also, there is no accessory plate; instead the edges of the valves are thickened and reflected to form a shield. At the hind end of the shell there is a black, horny piece which covers the base of the soft tube; the rest of the shell is greyish white. A piddock drills its tunnel by scraping away the soft rock with the roughened end of the shell, the bit of the drill. The two plates are gently rocked on the foot and the wavy ridges forced against the rock. The drilling position is gradually changed as the animal rotates, first clockwise, then anticlockwise. By doing this the tunnel or burrow is fashioned very evenly and smoothly. As the animal grows, so the burrow is deepened and widened. Piddocks are so specialized for their life, and it must therefore be a fairly safe one, that they cannot re-enter the rock if their burrows are destroyed.

Another shellfish which bores into soft rock, though it is quite different in appearance from the piddocks, is the date mussel, *Zelithophaga truncata* (Figure 68). Its common name is very apt, for it looks just

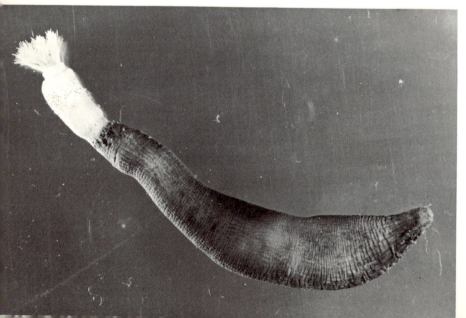

69. *Dendrostomum aeneum*, a peanut worm, with its introvert, the pale narrow end with the band of tiny spines and feathery tentacles, fully extended: it either makes its own tightly fitting burrow in mudstone or inhabits mud-filled piddock borings and crevices, and is often very common. Length, extended, up to 4 cm.

like a date. The shell is covered with a horny coat, violet brown in colour except for a stone grey segment at the rear (narrow) end. The date mussel probably bores by secreting a chemical of an acid nature. The opening of the burrow is very narrow; this is the animal's doing for it lines the outer part with spoil from the boring bound by a secretion. *Zelithophaga*, like other mussels, anchors itself firmly to the rock with a group of golden radiating threads, the byssus.

Shellfish are not the only borers into soft rock. Two worms also make themselves very neat homes. *Dendrostomum aeneum* (Figure 69), a peanut worm, is in shape rather like a Greek amphora (vase) without the handles. Its skin is very tough and wrinkled, and is orange brown in colour. From the front end a long, flexible pipe is shot out and withdrawn; at the tip of this pipe (called the introvert) is the mouth encircled by feathery tentacles. Just below the tip is a band of small spines; the function of these is not known, but possibly they are used like a file or sand paper to shape the burrow. *Dendrostomum* probably feeds on detritus, using the feathery crown to gather and sort the particles; however, the mechanism has yet to be studied. The other is a bristle worm, *Stylarioides parmatus* (Figure 70). The head end of this worm is fairly stout and carries a crown of long, slightly curved, iridescent bristles; these large bristles are surrounded below by two groups of shorter, finer bristles. Inside this 'palisade' of bristles is a group of slender, green filaments (gills) and a pair of white, grooved feelers (palps). The back of the head bears a thick, rough pad. The body is long and tapers gradually: the slender tail is normally held bent back along the stouter front part. This worm fits the burrow so tightly that it cannot be drawn out by the head without breaking. When the tide covers the burrow the bristly 'palisade' is protruded and splayed; the gills draw a current of water through the bristles and suspended particles are strained out, then removed by the palps and passed to the mouth.

Marphysa depressa (Figure 71), another bristle worm, is a common inhabitant of soft rock: the body is long and of a fairly uniform width, pinkish grey with short, simple or divided, red filaments (gills) along each side. Unlike *Stylarioides*, it does not have a neat home. *Marphysa* fashions a series of interconnecting galleries, mainly by enlarging tunnels left by other borers, though judging by the neatness of some of the channels it does appear to make a few of its own. This worm feeds on the remains of animals and the fronds of living seaweeds. It often emerges from its burrow when the tide is in or at ebb tide when the rock is damp, though seldom completely, retaining a hold on the burrow with its tail. Like the ragworm *Perinereis novaehollandiae* described earlier, *Marphysa* has a strong, muscular, protrusible pro- boscis armed with hard jaws which are used to handle, and tear the food.

Empty galleries are soon occupied by other animals, far too numerous for all of them to be mentioned here. Some of these 'squatters' are described elsewhere in this book: of these the commonest are the sea- anemone *Isactinia olivacea*, the half crab *Petrolisthes elongatus*, the ragworm *Perinereis novaehollandiae*, and the bristle worms *Timarete anchylochaeta* and *Terebella haplochaeta*. We just have not the space here to describe the others; however we will tell you that amongst the commonest are the two slipper limpets, *Maoricrypta costata* and *Maoricrypta monoxyla*, and the chinaman's hat, *Sigapatella novaezelan- diae*, all of which filter their food from the water, a flatworm, *Notoplana* sp., often seen as a gliding transparent film of living tissue, a hairy crab, *Pilumnus novaezelandiae*, and many different sea-mats and sponges which are all difficult to identify and are therefore best ignored.

---

10. Seaweeds. 1 is a brown, the rest are reds.

1. *Hormosira banksii*, 'Neptune's necklace', a brown seaweed which grows on flat or gently inclined faces and in pools on the lower half of the middle shore (also free living in mangrove swamps). Length up to 90 cm., extremely variable in size.

2. *Liagora harveyana*, an open rock species of the lower shore in moderately sheltered places on the open coast; the North Island only, sometimes dominant in the summer and autumn. Length to 7 cm.

3. *Pterocladia pinnata*, another lower shore species, chiefly a rock pool inhabitant though it occurs on rock in the shade; the North Island and northern South Island. Length up to 30 cm.

4. *Apophloea sinclairii,* grows on rock (not sandstone) of the middle shore, usually as a basal crust without projections; a North Island species, particularly prominent in the northern half. Greatest dimension up to 4 cm.

5. *Plocamium costatum*, occurs on rock at the lowest level of the shore and is particularly common in the North Island. Length up to 10 cm.

6. *Melanthalia abscissa*, a common low tidal species particularly on the open coast; found in the North Island (except in the SW.) and the Marlborough coast (the South Island). Length up to 20 cm.

7. *Gigartina circumcincta*, the leaf carrageen, a most prominent member of the lower shore algal belt on fairly exposed parts of the open coast. Length up to 25 cm.

8. *Champia novaezelandiae*, a low level species, occurring in the shade especially where water trickles across the rock, on the open coast. Length up to 12 cm.

9. *Laurencia thyrsifera* often grows in shallow tide pools carpeted with *Corallina officinalis* on platform reefs of the open coast; abundant in the summer. Length up to 5 cm.

Figure 10

7. *Stichaster australis*, the reef star, a conspicuous inhabitant of the lower shore along the exposed coast; in colour it varies from pinkish-brown to violet. Just over 90% of its food consists of the mussel *Perna canaliculus* which it eats when covered by the tide and digests when uncovered. Arm-spread up to 30 cm.

12. *Xenostrobus pulex,* the little black mussel, a zone forming species on rock which tolerates heavy waves, cloudy water and sand: it penetrates into harbours, living on wharf piles, the aerial roots of mangroves as well as open rock. Length up to 25 mm.

Figure 13

UNDER STONES AND ROCKS

The space beneath a stone or rock offers another special place where animals can hide, permanently or temporarily, away from the sun and wind when the tide is out and from predators when it is in, especially during the day. Not all loose rocks and stones offer satisfactory protection – that stones vary from being barren to carrying a luxuriant fauna is immediate proof of this. A large stone sited on the lower half of a shore in a fairly sheltered locality is quite obviously more habitable than a small stone at the same level on a shingle bank. The suitability of a loose stone or rock as a permanent home or retreat depends on the vertical position on the shore, size and texture, and the amount of local water movement. As with other special habitats, level on the shore determines the time available for feeding and breathing in water and, of course, the amount of water lost to the wind. Texture of the rock influences the settlement of the larvae (the young dispersal stages which are often very different in appearance to the adult animal), many kinds preferring a rough surface for attachment: size of the rock determines its stability, as does the strength of the water movement which also influences the replenishment of food and the amount of sediment settling out.

Most impressive to beginner and old-hand alike is the abundant, colourful and diverse life beneath a large rock sitting on the lower part of a shore where there is moderate wave action or a tidal current. One might call this the 'ideal' rock – all other kinds being less attractive though not less interesting. A similar rock in the quiet waters of the upper harbour will be heavily coated with mud and inhabited by those few animals which do not mind such conditions; in rough waters the same rock will be rolled about and serve only as a temporary home for a few nimble footed forms. Of course we are simplifying the picture greatly, for the rock on the sheltered shore may be supported well above the mud by other stones and offer quite clean living quarters below, and the rock on the exposed shore may only be shifted during the gale season, making a stable home for the rest of the year.

---

13. *Leptograpsus variegatus*, the large shore crab, a common inhabitant of the middle and upper shore of exposed rocky platforms. The male has larger pincers than the female. At night this crab moves out on to the open surface to feed on seaweed, small animals such as snails, and carrion. Occurs in the North Island and the northern half of the South Island. Width of the body up to 60 mm.

As one moves up the shore the variety of animals gradually decreases, though those which live at a higher level can often be very abundant. Just as we have seen with open rock, crevices and overhangs, at different levels one kind of animal is replaced by another, each succeeding one being a little better adapted to air conditions. High on the shore the sea animals finally surrender the habitat to a few terrestrial forms which do not mind a little splash or spray. Loose stones and rock, like seaweeds, crevices and overhangs, enable many sea animals to occupy the shore which they could not otherwise do.

Before describing the fauna beneath a loose rock we must draw your attention to the upper surface and sides, colonized, of course by organisms of the open rock. The top may be bare or occupied by barnacles, *Ralfsia* or *Corallina* depending on the level on the shore. Down the sides the organisms are zoned, just as on the open rock, except here the scale of banding is very reduced and temperature and light are the important controlling factors.

Under-stone species are very numerous indeed and their occurrence and grouping vary from one rock to another. Because of this, we have restricted our account to some of the common and most obvious inhabitants of a large rock in the lowest zone on a moderately sheltered shore (Figure 72), the 'ideal' type mentioned earlier. You must remember not to expect to find all of the species described here under any one rock or even on the same shore. Although none is rare, one or two of them may be hard to find.

On turning over the rock you may be startled by those animals which, when disturbed, jump, run or glide away. If you want to capture them for a closer examination you will need a small net or to be quick with your hands. After having perhaps caught and looked at one or two escapees you will turn your attention once again to the rock. You will immediately notice that the undersurface appears as though it has been used as a canvas by some modern artist for it is daubed with 'paint', pink, yellow and brown predominating, in some places thin, in others thick, often scumbled or glazed (Figure 73). Often the 'picture' has been turned into a collage by splodges of jelly and blancmange. On looking closely you will discover that these coloured patches are similar to the sort of thing you found on the overhang – they are sessile, colonial animals, collectively called 'marine growth' and we will consider them first.

All of the main types of plant-like animals which make up the 'marine growth' have been met with before in the sections on seaweeds and overhangs though many of the actual species are different. We will only

66

mention a very small number of these peculiar animals; the reason for this is that they are very difficult to identify, even for the biologist armed with his microscope and books on identification.

Here sponges are a very common component of the 'marine growth', often covering most of the undersurface of a rock. Two kinds of sponge are present. Commonest and most diverse is the substantial, complex type of sponge with a skeleton of siliceous spicules or horny fibres and an intricate system of tubes and chambers through which sea-water is driven; we met some of these under the overhang. One common species is *Microciona coccinea,* forming thin, small, dullish red patches with a velvety texture. The fawn and purple *Haliclona heterofibrosa* is another: it is much thicker and forms much larger patches and is raised here and there into cones or 'volcanoes'. The other type of sponge is small, compact and of simpler construction and shows little variety. The spaces within the body are simply organized, the 'flesh' is thin and the skeleton consists of calcareous spicules. *Leucosolenia* sp. (Figure 73) is one kind and is formed of compacted, branched tubes, bright green in colour. Another species is *Sycon ornatum* which looks like a pale yellow, miniature, globular cactus with a crown of long spines; like others of its kind, it is slightly more complex in internal structure than *Leucosolenia.*

Much of the undersurface of the rock is often covered with patches of 'paint' which is thin, and rough to the touch. These patches are sea-mats or polyzoans; the structure and feeding of these have been described in an earlier section. Many of the understone sea-mats, and there is a great number of them, are very tough indeed: the walls of the boxes which protect the soft parts are heavily impregnated with calcium carbonate; the 'roof' (upper side) is characteristically ornamented or sculptured.

Vying with the sponges and sea-mats for space on the rock are the sea-squirts, a group of animals which is particularly well represented on our rocky shores. The sea-squirts occur either as separate individuals, solitary or in groups, or as colonies of individuals embedded in a common coat, often arranged in a characteristic pattern. As mentioned earlier, sea-squirts feed by filtering out organic particles and minute organisms from the sea-water which is passed through the pharyngeal part of the gut. A common and easily recognizable example of the simple type of sea-squirt is *Corella eumyota* (Figure 73): it is oval in outline, somewhat flattened, and the fairly thick cartilage-like test is translucent, almost transparent, and the viscera show through as a reddish area. *Corella* lies attached by the right side to the rock; the mouth (oral siphon) is terminal and the other opening (atrial siphon) lies midway down the 'back'. *Didemnum candidum* (Figure 74), a sea-squirt of the compound sort, has the form of a thin, leathery (toughened by spicules of calcium carbonate) sheet, white, fawn or pink in colour, regularly pitted (star-shaped oral openings) with large openings (atrial siphons) evenly dispersed, each common to a group of individuals.

There is often tremendous competition between sponges, sea-mats and sea-squirts for living space on the undersurface of the rock. Usually the struggle is even, but occasionally one or other of these sedentary animals is very successful and takes over most of the surface, smothering other species in the process.

There are many other kinds of sedentary animal and sometimes one of them may dominate the undersurface of the rock. You may find a rock covered, often densely, with short, hard, pieces of white thread. These are the tubes of small bristle worms, very close relatives of *Pomatoceros caeruleus* which we described in the section on the open rock habitat. Fine, loosely coiled tubes are those of *Hydroides norvegica* which is easily recognized by the spiny crown atop the stopper (operculum) and the pink banded, feathery tentacles. The smaller tubes, coiled in a tight spiral, belong to *Spirorbis borealis* (Figure 73), a tiny species which has a disc-shaped stopper and a small number of yellow tentacles. *Spirorbis* can be particularly common on rocks a little higher on the shore where there is less competition for space from sponges, sea-mats and sea-squirts. Where the water is clear you may find solitary individuals of a large relative of these two worms, *Galeolaria hystrix* (Figure 75). The tube of this species has a crest which is double, wavy and spiny and ends in two sharply pointed spines above the aperture; it is white with pink and red near the opening. The animal is deep pinkish red and the gills and operculum are orange banded with white; the operculum bears several concentric rows of curved spines.

Bivalve molluscs, those expert filterers of food, are also present. One common species is the nesting mussel, *Ryenella impacta* (Figure 76): the shell is swollen and a trapezium in outline (from the side), each valve is ribbed at the front and rear with a smooth zone in between; it is olive brown and has a low gloss. Like the other mussels, it attaches itself to the rock by a group of strong threads (the byssus); however, *Ryenella* takes thread-making further than the others, for it weaves and wraps itself within a loosely woven blanket.

Deserving a mention here are three very striking sessile animals, all

68

present under stones where the sea is clear and moves briskly. *Tetraclita purpurescens*, a barnacle, is a flattened cone of four finely and irregularly ribbed plates which are honeycombed internally: *Stephopoma roseum* is a small snail whose pinkish shell is easily mistaken for that of a tube worm like *Spirorbis* – it too feeds by filtering; finally, *Flabellum rubrum*, a fan coral, which is so similar in structure to the closely related sea-anemones except for the large, calcareous protective cup and very delicate body.

The mobile animals which live under stones and rocks fall roughly into two groups: (1) those which spend all or most of their time under the rock even when it is immersed and (2) those which only shelter there at low tide and emerge to work the open rock, with limpets and top shells, when covered by the sea.

The permanent or semi-permanent dwellers, by far the largest of the two groups, are best considered by what they eat. Having given some space above to a description of the sessile animals, perhaps you will be wondering whether this apparently appetizing and abundant fare is eaten. In fact it is, but not as intensively as you might expect.

Most striking amongst the predators of sessile organisms are the sea-slugs – they are often very gaudy and bizarre in appearance. Although there are many different kinds, only a few are encountered regularly. *Dendrodoris citrina* (Figure 77) is a large common species, pale yellow to orange speckled with opaque white, elliptical in outline and pustulate, with a pair of retractile horns (tentacles) at the front end and a circlet of feathery gills at the back. It certainly looks a tasty morsel for a gull or fish, but it is not, for it is well protected by the glands in the skin of the back which produce a nasty tasting substance. *Dendrodoris* feeds on sponges, possibly sea-squirts as well; first it makes a hole in the protective layers of the prey's body with saliva, working this with the long sausage-shaped proboscis, and then dissolves and sucks up the soft insides. Another common sea-slug of the same type is *Rostanga rufescens*, much smaller than *Dendrodoris* and red and rough. Unlike *Dendrodoris*, *Rostanga* feeds on thin, encrusting red sponges such as *Microciona coccinea* which it scrapes off with its toothed tongue.

Our largest side-gilled sea-slug is *Pleurobranchaea novaezelandiae* (Figure 78); it has a soft, puckered grey skin, a wide, angled veil and a pair of small, scroll-like tentacles at the front end, a long, feathery gill on the right side and a thin internal shell. It is a voracious carnivore, and although it has a liking for sea-squirts which it quickly penetrates with its proboscis and sharply toothed tongue, it is fairly catholic and will attack many other soft bodied animals.

69

Another sea-slug, of quite a different kind, is *Phidiana militaris* (Figure 79); it has a long, slender but deep body with two pairs of horns (tentacles) at the front end and rows of cigar-shaped processes along the back; the body is translucent white and the second pair of tentacles and the top of the head are orange and the core of the back-processes reddish brown. This slug feeds on hydroids and, quite astonishingly, the unused stinging cells of the food organism are lodged in special sacs opening at the tips of the back-processes and used for the slug's protection, exploding when it is molested.

A carnivorous snail *Lamellaria ophione* (Figure 80) is like a sea-slug at first sight. It is very slippery to the touch; the back is smooth except for a few short irregular processes and varies from pale yellow to bright orange, often dappled with brown. *Lamellaria* is easily distinguished from sea-slugs; it is very firm because of the hard internal shell, the skirt of the back is folded at the front to form a tube through which water is drawn into the gill cavity and the single pair of tentacles are long and narrow. *Lamellaria* feeds on sea-squirts which it tears with its toothed tongue. Yet another predator of sessile animals is *Typosyllis brachycola*, a bristle worm which feeds on the soft parts of hydroids and possibly other types of 'marine growth'. It is a smallish, delicate worm, easily recognized by its colour; the head is orange and the rest green except for a small intervening zone of purple (part of the proboscis which shows through the transparent body). *Odontosyllis polycera* (Figure 81) is a very close relative of *Typosyllis*; larger and more robust, it is easily recognized by the closely spaced hoops, alternately colourless and dark bluish grey, the heart-shaped flap, which extends forwards over the head, and the simple filaments along the sides (in *Typosyllis* each of these filaments, sensory structures, is like a chain of beads).

Another carnivorous bristle worm, though it scavenges as well, is the scale worm *Lepidonotus polychroma* (Figure 82). The body is short, flat and flexible (permits the worm to squeeze into all sorts of small chinks and depressions in the rock), and is protected above by twelve pairs of over-lapping plates, speckled with brown pigment; two long, slender processes (palps) and three shorter tentacles project at the anterior end. Food, living or dead, is grasped, crushed and ingested with the short, protrusible proboscis or throat, armed with four small, horny jaws.

Now to those carnivores which feed mainly on mobile prey. The flatworm *Thysanozoon brochii* feeds on small snails, worms and shrimp-like crustaceans which it entangles in mucus and then engulfs through a large, frilly, trumpet-shaped proboscis. *Thysanozoon* (Figure 83) is one of our largest marine flatworms and is quickly recognized by the 'horns' at the front end and the short processes, rather like those of the sea-slug *Phidiana*, which cover its back. This flatworm is fawn spotted with black and reddish brown. When dislodged it swims, not very efficiently, by vigorously flapping the sides of its body. Other soft-bodied predators are the ribbon worms and bristle worms of various kinds – different species to those described elsewhere but feeding in the same way.

The whelks, close relatives of the rock shells, such prominent carnivores of the open rock habitat, should be mentioned here, though they probably eat carrion as often as living prey (snails, bivalves and worms are probably the animals most frequently attacked). One of these whelks is *Buccinulum heteromorphum* (Figure 84): the shell is a neat spire, with fairly fine spiral ridges and closely set, low ribs, and a short groove at the base for the breathing tube (siphon); it is white, broken by lines of pink and dark violet. The body is white with dark brown pigment on the upper parts. There are other whelks, some quite large and attractive in shape and colour; also, there are many more carnivorous snails, some very small such as the margin shells.

Most determined of the under-stone carnivores are the two cushion stars, *Patiriella regularis* and *Stegnaster inflatus*. *Patiriella* (Figure 85) is rough to the touch and when immersed is covered with small, thin-walled bladders called papulae, which are respiratory structures; it is usually bluish green in colour with brown crescent-shaped plates. *Stegnaster* (Figure 86) is less rough, and is membranous and almost a perfect pentagon (the sides are straight, not indented as in *Asterina*); its colour is very variable, it can be pale orange blotched with red and black or pale and bright purple or cream daubed with red, blue, green or brown. Of all marine animals, starfish and their relatives (sea-urchins, brittle-stars and sea-cucumbers) come closest to the science fiction writers' space monster – they are geometrical in shape, usually heavily armoured and weaponed, mechanical in movement, and the predacious forms are hard to deter from attack and have an insatiable appetite. Like sea-urchins and sea-cucumbers, starfish move with a steady tread, but with more purpose and faster – hardly surprising though since they are active predators. The rows of tube feet in the radiating grooves on the undersurface (the mouth lies at the centre) are used as in the sea-urchin (described in the section on rock pools); individual feet are extended, attached and shortened, pulling the animal along. Although the feet step in one direction, there is no regular sequence of movement of adjacent feet. The prey is almost any animal which is not quick enough to escape the clutches of the cushion star; snails, small bivalves and bristle worms are the most frequently eaten prey. When the prey animal is trapped beneath the cushion star, the back is arched and the stomach everted, pressed against the soft parts of the victim and digestion started. As soon as the prey is reduced to a broth it is drawn into the body with the stomach. Any hard parts swallowed are disgorged later.

Liveliest of the carnivores are the shore fish. One of the largest and commonest is the rockfish, *Acanthoclinus quadridactylus* (Figure 87), which is not the least bit easy to catch even when the rocks are high and dry. It is strong and slippery and remains very active out of water; when disturbed it leaps about amongst the rocks in an effort to find another sanctuary. The second pair of fins are strong and finger-like and

---

24. *Haustrum haustorium*, the dark rock shell. Though never very common, a few individuals are present on most reefs in moderate shelter. It lives on the lower half of the shore, sheltering in clefts at ebb tide. *Haustrum* feeds on snails including its relative the oyster borer (*Lepsiella scobina*). Height (of the shell) up to 6 cm.

25. *Obelia longissima*, a hydroid: part of a colony growing on the frond of the flapjack (*Carpophyllum maschalocarpum*). The feeding-heads jut out at regular intervals along the upright 'shoots'. During the breeding season little jellyfish (called medusae) are released by the hydroid — these jellyfish swim and feed in the surface waters (they are temporary members of the plankton). The jellyfish (each is either male or female) shed sex cells which fuse and develop into a larva (a special young stage) which seeks out a suitable place to settle and grows into a new hydroid colony. Height (of the 'shoot') up to 25 mm.

26. (Right) *Staurocladia hodgsoni*, a hydroid jellyfish, anchored (right way up i.e. with the mouth downwards) by suckers (at the tip of special branches of the tentacles) to the frond of the kelp *Ecklonia radiata*. The tentacles with swellings (batteries of nematocysts) are waved about to catch prey: when a small animal is caught it is thrust under the body and into the mouth. Diameter up to 4 mm.
(Left) *Cricophorus nutrix*, a small sea-anemone; a young individual (no brood chamber) attached to the frond of the flapjack (*Carpophyllum maschalocarpum*). Including the tentacles, up to 15 mm. across.

27. *Hippothoa bougainvillei*, a sea-mat or polyzoan; a colony growing on the frond of the kelp, *Ecklonia radiata*. The conspicuous round swellings with an opaque centre are the ovicells, special compartments in which the larvae (one in each ovicell) are brooded. On hatching, the larvae swim about searching for a suitable surface on which to settle and start a new colony. *Hippothoa* also grows on the seaweed *Sargassum sinclairii* and on stones and shells. Diameter of colony up to 25 mm.

72

14. *Sypharochiton pelliserpentis*, the snake's skin chiton, is often very common on the open surface or in pools of the middle shore on soft and hard rocky reefs ranging from the turbulent open coast to quiet harbour waters. The valves of this chiton are roughened by erosion (may bear small seaweeds or barnacles) except in the small, prettily coloured form, *S. p. sinclairii*, which lives on the lower shore along wave battered coasts. Whether living in pools or on open rock, this chiton seems to feed only when covered by the tide. Length up to 30 mm.

23. *Neothais scalaris*, the white rock shell (some individuals have a light brown shell with prominent ribs). This rock shell is particularly common where the mussel *Perna canaliculus* forms a dense belt. On sheltered reefs, where this mussel is sparse, *Neothais* attacks and eats the cat's eye. A northern species, in the South Island its place is taken by a relative, *Lepsithais lacunosus*. Height (of the shell) up to 11 cm.

Figure 24 See facing page

Figure 25 See facing page

Figure 26 See facing page

Figure 27 See facing page

28. *Thoristella oppressa*, a small top shell which is quite common on the fronds of the flapjack (*Carpophyllum maschalocarpum*) and the kelp (*Ecklonia radiata*) and on the undersurfaces of rocks where the water is clear and the reef moderately sheltered from waves. Occurs in the North Island and northern South Island. Height (of the shell) up to 6 mm.

29. *Micrelenchus dilatatus*, a small top shell which, like *Thoristella*, is quite common on large seaweeds of the lower shore. This specimen has a plain-coloured shell. Height (of the shell) up to 8 mm.

30. *Trochus viridis*, the greenish top shell: this snail lives with *Micrelenchus* and *Thoristella*, but is never common. The shell of this specimen is partly covered with barnacles, a tiny tube worm and a sea-squirt. Height (of the shell) up to 20 mm.

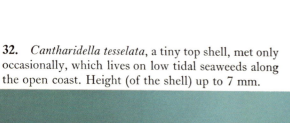

32. *Cantharidella tesselata*, a tiny top shell, met only occasionally, which lives on low tidal seaweeds along the open coast. Height (of the shell) up to 7 mm.

31. *Cantharidus purpuratus*, a rather uncommon top shell which lives on kelp in clear water along the coast of the North Island and northern South Island. Height (of the shell) up to 25 mm.

33. *Hippolyte bifidirostris*, a chameleon prawn, quickly identified by its humped back, large rostrum (beak-like projection at the front end of the body) and prominent eyes; it occurs in moderate numbers amongst large seaweeds at low tide. Length up to 4 cm.

34. *Amphoroidea falcifer*, an isopod crustacean which is easily identified by its shape; the axe-like front end is formed from enlarged basal segments of the first pair of feelers (properly called antennules). *Amphoroidea* lives on the kelp *Ecklonia radiata*, maintaining a firm hold on the frond with the strong claws and toothed pads at the tips of its seven pairs of walking legs. It swims powerfully using the paddle-like rear limbs (the pleopods). The surface layers of the kelp on which *Amphoroidea* feeds are cut with the jaws and thrust into the mouth with other special feeding limbs. Length up to 15 mm.

36. *Phlyctenactis tuberculosa*, the wandering sea-anemone; usually quite rare floating amongst seaweed at low tide or in deep rock pools in sheltered places on the eastern side of the North Island and north eastern part of the South Island. Height up to 15 cm.

37. *Notomithrax ursus*, the hairy seaweed crab, lives amongst seaweeds at low tide mark and in large pools higher up the shore. Hydroids sea-mats and sea-squirts are sometimes used with, or instead of, seaweeds for camouflage. This seaweed crab can be distinguished from two close relatives (Peron's Seaweed crab, *Notomithrax peroni*, and the lesser Seaweed crab, *Notomithrax minor*) by the spiny ridges on two segments (fourth segment or 'wrist' and fifth or 'arm') of the pincer. Width of body up to 38 mm.

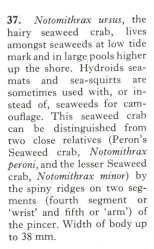

38. *Cookia sulcata*, Cook's turban, a relative of the cat's eye. *Cookia* favours clear waters; large individuals live on rock at low tide mark where they feed on encrusting calcareous red seaweeds, small ones on the flapjack (*Carpophyllum maschalocarpum*): it is not common. Height (of the shell) up to 9 cm.

40. The shallow part, containing loose stones and rocks, of a large rock pool (about 0·5 m. i.e. knee deep, at the deepest part) of the lower shore on a wave protected section of the open coast: the seaweeds are *Carpophyllum plumosum* (centre, right side), *Sargassum sinclairii* (one plant, just above the centre) and *Corallina officinalis* (centre, bottom); the animals are the sea egg, *Evechinus chloroticus* (one, above and slightly to the left of the centre), the sea hare (*Aplysia dactylomela* (one, a little to the left of the sea egg), the cushion star *Patiriella regularis* (three, below the sea egg and sea hare) and the cat's eye, *Lunella smaragda* (several, scattered about the pool).

act both as props and stilts: the body is flattened from side to side, a useful adaptation for fitting into narrow cracks and spaces, and is black marked with white. *Acanthoclinus* is not very fussy about what it eats – most prominent in its diet are small crabs, isopods, barnacles and chitons.

As elsewhere in nature, carnivores tend to be rather wasteful, often leaving a meal partially eaten. Added to this, animals die through disease or old age and their bodies lie about rotting. These remains are food for another group, the scavengers or 'cleaning department'. Most important scavengers are the large crustacea, the prawns, crabs and allies, which use their pincers to cut or tear the carcass, or to hold it for the jaws and other mouth parts.

Alope spinifrons (Figure 88), a prawn, is common where the water is clear; like *Palaemon*, described in the section on rock pools, it is alert, nimble and very quick, darting away to a dark corner when disturbed. This prawn is immediately recognized by its colour; it is bluish green with stripes of orangish red along the body and bands of purplish red on the legs. When feeding it is very genteel; the fine pincers are used deftly to snip, lift or hold pieces of food. *Alope* also eats amphipods and filamentous seaweeds.

The crabs are the 'heavy brigade' amongst the scavengers. Their pincers are large and blunt, and used to hold and tear rather than cut. Likening them to the fine scissor-like sort of the prawn, those of the crab are heavy duty wire clippers. Most spritely of the crabs living beneath rocks is the common rock crab, *Hemigrapsus edwardsi* (Figure 89); its body is squarish, sharply toothed at the front corners, and purple marked with black, brown and yellow. Not so common, slow moving, rather dull-witted by comparison with *Hemigrapsus*, are the New Zealand cancer crab, *Cancer novaezelandiae* (Figure 90), and the black finger crab, *Ozius truncatus* (Figure 91). *Cancer novaezelandiae* is a close relative of the European edible crab, though much smaller; it is short-legged with a broad, rounded body, fluted along the edge like a pie crust, and reddish brown with dark brown tips to the knobbly pincers. It is a very docile crab, sitting motionless when uncovered or when held in the hand. *Ozius* is of a stronger build and is much less tranquil in temperament, and will give its incautious captor a very nasty nip. It is dull reddish brown with black nippers. In the clear waters of the open coast you may find the triangular crab, *Eurynolambrus australis* (Figure 92): the body has the shape of an isosceles triangle with a wide base, the limbs are short and angular in section and the pincers fairly long and finely

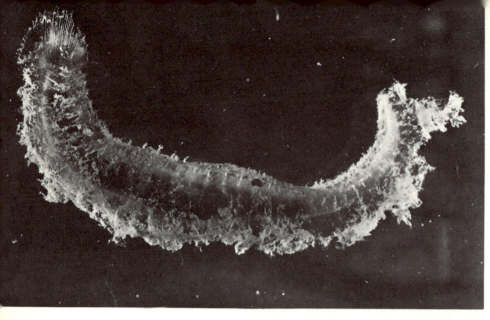

95. *Flabelligera affinis*, a bristle worm of the lower shore, is commonest under stones on reefs in moderately sheltered places. It is easily recognized by the thick gelatinous coat (often with fine debris adhering to it) and the stout feeding bristles encircling the head end. Length up to 7 cm.

pointed. *Eurynolambrus* is one of our most attractive crabs, being mottled red and brown with purple and white nippers. Living higher on the shore is the big-hand crab, *Heterozius rotundifrons* (Figure 93). *Heterozius* is smooth, elliptical and bluish grey with patches of yellow and as it remains very still when uncovered, it is easily mistaken for a pebble. Shape of the claws distinguishes the sexes; in the female they are long and slender, in the male the right is swollen.

Most abundant of all crabs on the lower half of a sheltered shore is the common half crab, *Petrolisthes elongatus* (Figure 94). It has very large nippers for its little round body and is very agile even out of water. *Petrolisthes* is not a true crab – it is related to hermit crabs, ghost shrimps and squat lobsters. The relationship is betrayed by the long feelers and tail fan at the tip of the abdomen which is normally held folded beneath the body. The last pair of legs are very small and are held raised – these are used for cleaning the gills, not walking. *Petrolisthes* feeds as other crabs do, by scavenging; also, it sweeps the water with the hairy last pair of mouth appendages straining out small particles of debris which are then passed to the mouth by the other small feeding appendages.

Scavengers do not always do a thorough job for small scraps of food are missed or swept aside during feeding or, because they are light, are carried away by local currents to settle nearby. Small particles of organic matter accumulate under stones and rocks where the force of the waves is dampened, or they become fixed to rough growths or sticky patches. This 'dust' is swept up and eaten by other animals. One of these 'sweepers' is the bristle worm *Flabelligera affinis* (Figure 95). The body is short, bright green and protected by a thick gelatinous coat. At the front end are two semi-circles of long bristles: like its relative *Stylarioides*, these are used to collect particles which are transferred to the mouth by a pair of grooved palps. Unlike *Stylarioides*, *Flabelligera* moves about

74

rather like a caterpillar, and as it does, brushes up particles with the front bristles. Other bristle worms which gather up fine particles, particularly those related to *Terebella*, are commonly found under stones.

Several chitons or coat-of-mail shells (shell of eight articulating plates) live under stones and rocks, feeding on the film of debris as well as minute plants. *Ischnochiton maorianus* (Figure 96) is often very abundant: it is long and fairly narrow and the eight plates are smooth, so is the thin, leathery girdle or skirt (the scales covering it are minute). So variable is its colour that it is impossible to give an adequate description here: the girdle may be grey or black, uniform or mottled and the plates of the shell green and pink, orange brown with purple peaks, or raw sienna and white stripes, but there are many other colours and

103. *Haliotis iris*, the paua or mutton-fish: two specimens with head and body tentacles extended. This shellfish lives under rocks and boulders at low tide mark on the open coast. Much sought after for its meat and shell, the paua is now only common on little-frequented parts of the coast. The paua is quickly distinguished from two other native species of *Haliotis*, *H. australis* (hihiwa karariwha) and *H. virginea* by the prominent lip which runs part way around the shell. Length up to 14 cm.

104. *Scutus breviculus*, the ducksbill limpet or rori. This snail is quite frequent under rocks of the lower shore in harbour waters. Length up to 15 cm.

patterns. This chiton is perhaps the fastest moving of all the local species; when you turn over a rock it quickly crawls around to the other side. *Ischnochiton* feeds at night, moving out on to the sides to graze there. Although it occurs in the clear water of the open coast, it only dwells where the water movement is reduced, for it has poor powers of adhering to the rock. Very sheltered shores are also inhabited by this chiton; it will even occupy stones and rocks partly embedded in muddy sand. As frequent in occurrence as *Ischnochiton*, though never quite so numerous, is *Amaurochiton glaucus* (Figure 97). It is broader and sturdier than *Ischnochiton* and clings much more firmly to the rock; also, *Amaurochiton* seems to endure a wider range of shore conditions since it can live in rock pools (low on the shore, deep, often fringed with *Carpophyllum*), on reefs well inside a harbour and on wave battered boulder beaches. The conspicuously scaly girdle and the shell-plates are glossy and the colour and pattern of both quite variable, though not approaching the array of 'dress' displayed by *Ischnochiton*. Usually it is blue or green; if patterned, then the markings are frequently brown. *Amaurochiton* often extends up the shore to near the mean tide level. *Notoplax violacea* (Figure 98) is a much less common chiton – you will be fortunate to see more than one or two individuals during a low tide. It is a species which seems to prefer semi-sheltered shores where the water is fairly clear. The girdle is wide and fleshy, orange sometimes dappled with brown, and there are little groups of bristles close to the plates. The plates are marked with brown, in a fine criss-cross pattern, and violet.

Brittle-stars are also 'cleaners'. Their name is very apt; great care must be exercised when picking up one for they are quick to shed pieces of arm. Brittleness, however, does not mean weakness; these animals have considerable strength (you will soon become aware of this if you cage one in your hands). Like the starfishes, brittle-stars have tube feet, but these are not tipped with suckers, nor are they used in moving. The brittle-star levers itself along with the five long mobile arms (sharply separated from the small disc-like body), using the spines (when present) to grip the bottom. These are the fastest of all echinoderms. The brittle-star scrapes up small particles of organic matter with the toothed jaws or catches them with mucus which is then carried to the mouth by the tube feet. Two largish species common in the clear water of the open coast are the dark purple *Ophiopteris antipodum* (Figure 99), which has very long, flattened arm spines, and the grey and white banded *Ophionereis fasciata* (Figure 100), which has short spines.

Playing a part in cleaning up the fine debris is the little sea-cucumber *Ocnus brevidentis*, a minute relative of the huge beche-de-mer of tropical reefs. *Ocnus* (Figure 101) is cylindrical with five rows of tube feet running along the body; it is hard to the touch due to the calcareous plates in the skin and is pinkish white spotted with red and brown. The mouth lies at the centre of the circle of tentacles at the front end of the body; these tentacles are sticky with mucus and each in turn is dipped into the debris, then thrust into the mouth and licked clean. Sometimes you will find a large species of sea-cucumber named *Stichopus mollis* (Figure 102): the skin is soft and thick (yellowish brown or dark brown above and cream and yellowish brown below); the upper surface of the body is raised into conical protruberances of varying size and on the lower there are three tracts of tube feet (organs of locomotion and attachment as in the starfish and sea-urchin). There are twenty tentacles around the mouth, each with a cup-like tip formed by a circlet of small processes; each tentacle is used like a scoop, not as a sticky 'mop-head' as in *Ocnus*.

Some of the animals one finds beneath a rock only hide there when it is light or the tide is out. At other times they roam about the shore at the same level feeding. One of these animals is the famous paua, *Haliotis iris* (Figure 103), recognized by its dull, ear-shaped shell perforated by a curved row of holes, the exits for the respiratory current which enters the gill chamber at the sides of the body. Few New Zealanders need reminding about the beauty of the inner surface of the shell; the bright iridescent nacre is much used for jewellery and as an inlay ornamenting wooden goods of various kinds. The soft body is black: the head bears a pair of long, stout tentacles and the skirt a row of long, fine processes which poke out under the shell when the animal is on the move. Accompanying the paua is another snail, the ducksbill limpet, *Scutus breviculus* (Figure 104), similar in size and colour, but with a much reduced shell, a small shield hidden in a pocket at the top of the body. Like the paua, *Scutus* emerges from beneath the rock when the tide is in to graze on small delicate seaweeds. A third shellfish emerging to graze is the large, long and narrow, rather rubbery chiton, *Cryptoconchus porosus* (Figure 98). You may be surprised to learn that *Cryptoconchus* is a chiton, for there seems to be no sign of the eight piece shell. However, it is like all other chitons; lying within the skin are the eight plates, a very pretty bluish green, their positions marked by the paired conical swellings along the upper surface. *Cryptoconchus* may be bluish green, orange or brown, sometimes mottled with darker pigment. Commoner than either the paua or ducksbill limpet, and possibly *Cryptoconchus* too, is the eleven armed starfish, *Coscinasterias calamaria* (Figure 105). The upper surface of this starfish, which is generally brown with the arms banded with bluish grey, is unlike any of the others we have described for it bears rows of short spikey table-like structures giving it a very prickly appearance. *Coscinasterias* is one of the most irresistible predators of the lower shore. It eats barnacles, crabs, sea-urchins, chitons and bivalves. Like *Stichaster*, the prey is never swallowed whole; the stomach is everted and spread over the victim, unless it is a bivalve mollusc, in which case the stomach is inserted through the narrow opening.

Shores of Sand and Mud

INTRODUCTION

The beach is the part of the shore which people visit most frequently. It is more attractive than rock: it slopes gently and evenly and makes an easy entrance to the sea for swimming, it is kind to the feet, safe for the children to play on and with, and comfortable for adults to sit or lie on. Those who love the beach and visit it often probably think they know it well. But do they? Most of them would tell you that, unlike the rocky reef, the beach is almost lifeless. Probably the only organisms they would identify with the beach would be the hordes of nasty flies and the occasional earwig of the backshore which harass the picnic party, the now rather rare delicacy, the toheroa, and other edible shell-fish of lower rank, the tuatua, pipi and tuangi (cockle), and those dead and dying plants and animals along the strand line which mostly come from other parts of the coast or the open sea.

But the beach abounds with life of great variety, all tucked away below the surface when the tide is out. To find the inhabitants you will have to dig over the beach with a fork: to make a quick and easy capture you need to wash and shake the clods through a garden sieve (1/8" mesh). You may wonder why animals and plants do not live on the surface: the reason is simple, the surface is continually shifted about by the waves and currents, and the wind when the tide is out, and offers no stable base for attachment. Without a firm grip on the bottom the organism would be rolled about and be quite unable to make a living. Only when a stone or a large piece of shell is firmly bedded in the beach or there is an outcrop of rock will you find permanent surface dwellers – creatures which are typically found on a reef. Even so, the species are few which will tolerate scouring by sand on a surf beach or smothering by silt on a mud flat. One such example is the little black mussel *Xenostrobus pulex* which does not seem to mind being temporarily buried in, or abraded by, sand; another is the barnacle *Elminius modestus* which seems willing to suffer turbid waters and a film of silt. Since a subterranean life is necessary for survival on a beach, the plants which predominate are dinoflagellates and diatoms, minute relatives of the seaweeds which can

80

42. *Pagurus novaezelandiae*, a hermit crab. A very common inhabitant of rocky shores, particularly mud filmed harbour reefs; at high tide it roams freely over the shore, at low tide it retreats into pools. This hermit crab feeds mainly on the organic matter in the sediment which collects on the reef. Living and moribund snails are also eaten, the hermit crab using its pincers to kill and dismember the prey. Width of the body up to 16 mm.

39. *Hippocampus abdominalis*, the seahorse. This photograph is of a female: the male is distinguished by the spines on the top of the head, the smooth 'belly' or brood pouch and the anal fins being closer to the head (would mark the position of the navel if it had one). As in many other bony fish, the seahorse is supported by a buoyancy tank, the air bladder, and by increasing or decreasing the volume of gas in this it can move up or down. Length up to 30 cm.

41. *Evechinus chloroticus*, the sea-egg. The sea egg is most abundant below extreme low tide mark, often congregating to form groups of up to a thousand individuals: the sea-egg wanders about mainly at night, though the distances covered must be very small (total for a year may be less than 4 m.). Man is not the only predator of the sea-egg; it is eaten by the snapper, large starfish and the trumpet shell (*Charonia capax*). Diameter of the test up to 11 cm.

43. *Palaemon affinis*, the common prawn, inhabits reefs, muddy sand beaches and harbour banks. It feeds at night, moving up the shore with the flood tide and is often stranded in pools by the ebb. As well as feeding on decaying plants, its principal food, and animals, it also eats diatoms (microscopic plants), the green seaweed *Enteromorpha*, and living animals such as opossum shrimps, amphipods and recently settled barnacles. Length up to 75 mm.

44. *Isocradactis magna*, a large sea-anemone, is fairly common in pools along the open coast. Including the tentacles, up to 12 cm. across.

46. A small pool of the upper shore on the open (East) coast: the seaweeds are *Chaetomorpha linum* (the dense, dark green growth), *Enteromorpha* sp. (the sparse, yellowish green filaments above the *Chaetomorpha*) and *Corallina officinalis* (purplish pink, bushy plants, one at the centre, another where the *Chaetomorpha* ends on the left); the animals are the white rock shell, *Neothais scalaris* (yellowish shell at the centre), the bristle worm *Pomatoceros caeruleus* (several specimens, with their blue arms showing, down the left side), the small horn shell *Zeacumantus subcarinatus* and the blue-banded periwinkle, *Littorina unifasciata* (small shells scattered about the pool).

live between the particles at the surface where there is still sufficient light for photosynthesis.

There are a great many different kinds of beach (using the term in a broad sense), ranging from very coarse sand on the open coast to the sticky mud of the harbour or estuary. What determines the nature of a beach is the strength of local water movement, i.e., waves and currents which are in turn governed by the shape of the surrounding land, and the type of sediment available – we will say more about this when we describe the principal kinds of beach.

Since, with few exceptions (see shores of mud), the animals and plants hide within the beach, you will wonder what is the influence on them of such 'climatic' elements as the tide, waves, sun and wind which are so important on the rocky shore. The tide controls the length of time for feeding, and to a lesser extent, breathing, but not drying out as the beach remains wet between tides, water being held between the particles. Unlike on open rock, the action of the waves is indirect, though none the less important; the waves move and fashion the deposit which is the home of these organisms. The size of the particles which make up the beach is very important since it controls the amount of water held and its circulation. The amount of contained water is also important in burrowing: if there is too little present to fill the spaces between the particles enlarged by the digging animal, the sediment becomes dry, stiff and very hard to move; if there is too much water, agitation floats more particles making the sediment wet, soft and very easy to burrow through. The contained water protects the organisms against drying out; the vertical level of the water, and consequently the organisms, depend on the holding power (capillarity) of the sediment, being low with coarse particles (large spaces) and high with fine (small spaces). Good water circulation is vital if there is to be adequate replenishment of oxygen for breathing; it is highest in coarse deposits where the water holding power is low and vice versa, even when the tide covers the beach (lower layers may lack oxygen).

Sun and wind are not very important: although the top layers of the beach may be heated or dried when the tide is out the animals can retreat below this to where conditions remain relatively unchanged. There is, of course, the danger that surface water of increased temperature or saltiness (due to evaporation) would be drawn down by the movements, particularly respiratory, of the animals. However, discomfort or death is avoided by the animal shutting down its activity whilst the conditions at the surface are adverse.

Reef and Beach Life of New Zealand

Fine particles of organic matter, important as food everywhere in the sea, have a great influence on animals which live in a beach. The quantity of such particles settling out depends on water movement and is naturally greatest in quiet waters. Such conditions of plenty can make a rather disagreeable habitat of the deeper levels; fine particles clog the spaces between the larger ones, greatly reducing water (and oxygen) circulation; bacteria acting on this organic matter use up the available oxygen, hydrogen sulphide is formed, then iron oxide is converted to sulphide and this blackens the deposit. This black layer, present on all beaches, is therefore an excellent indicator of living conditions. On a mud flat where huge quantities of organic matter are laid down the black layer is close to the surface; on a surf beach where very little settles it lies deep.

Since the organisms are protected by the deposit from the sun and wind, let in by the receding tide, you would expect them to have a fairly even distribution. However, this is not so. Like the organisms on rock, those of the beach are zoned. This zonation is, however, principally caused by the differing periods of time needed by the organisms for feeding (collecting nutrient salts in the case of the tiny plants) and aquatic breathing and by a changing grain size. Average particle size increases up the beach. The reason for this is that the swash of a broken wave has enough energy to carry a certain sized particle up, but the backwash has not enough to bring it down (some of the energy having been lost by the sea draining back through the deposit). To discover this zonation for yourself will mean having to do a fair amount of systematic digging and counting of individuals of the common species. You will discover that three primary zones (Figure 106) can be recognized and that these seem to be related to the monthly tidal cycle (at least more so than the zones of the rocky shore). These zones are: (1) upper shore, occupied by those species which are only covered by the sea briefly at spring tides; (2) middle shore, by those species which need daily periods of immersion and emersion; and (3) lower shore, by those which can only withstand infrequent, short periods of emersion. After working out the distributions of the very common species, you will see that the bands are not perfectly even like those on open rock; these organisms are mobile and consequently their zones are made rather ragged by their individual movements. You must not expect the zonal pattern produced by your digging to be representative of the whole beach: often the sediments of a beach form a patchwork (water movement is never perfectly even); this is particularly true of a harbour beach. Also, you will only come to know the faunal pattern of a particular beach if you watch it all through the year; waves, currents, streams and rivers change with the seasons and so, as a consequence, does the structure of the beach.

Since there are a great many types of beach, differing in the mixture of shell, sand, silt, clay and organic matter, and a large number of organisms, we can only select, as we have had to do so with rock, a few examples to demonstrate the important features of the beach as a habitat and where and how a few of the common inhabitants live. We shall describe first a sandy beach, i.e., one where sand particles predominate, then we shall go to the other extreme, a mud flat, and finally, a beach of muddy sand where the good and bad features of the other two are balanced.

SAND

Beaches of coarse sand (Figure 107) occupy long stretches of the coast. These beaches are steep, clean, smooth and very firm. They are the least rewarding of beaches for the effort needed to study them. The list of inhabitants is small; obviously few animals have become adapted to coping with the difficult living conditions which such a beach offers. But there is still considerable variety amongst the few inhabitants. It is easy to understand why the life of such a beach is so limited. Heavy waves continually shift the surface layers, and at times so do strong winds: this means that the large animals have to continually re-embed themselves or at least repair their temporary burrows. Such wild conditions offer little scope to the animal which makes a permanent burrow. Little water is held by the deposit though this does not matter so much in terms of the organisms drying out since the swash of the breakers periodically reaches high to keep most of the beach moist. The deposit is extremely hard to dig because of the low water content and large size of the particles; but such firmness makes it easy to crawl on. Little organic matter is present and water (and oxygen) circulation is high; as a result the black layer lies deep. A low organic content means that large animals which feed by eating the deposit are rare.

Sandy beaches often change remarkably during the year. Spilling breakers of the settled, quieter seasons lay down the particles evenly; in the stormy periods, particularly of winter, this good work is undone as the wave shape is changed to that of the destructive plunging breaker

107.   Home of the toheroa — a sandy beach (on the west coast of the North Island) exposed to, and formed by, the prevailing south-westerly wind and oceanic swell. The beach is about 200 m. wide (at EXTREME LOW WATER SPRINGS) and has a uniform and gradual slope except for a slightly steeper section immediately in front of the small hills (of breccia). In spring the heavy bloom of phytoplankton (minute drifting plants) is left as a thin layer of slime by the receding tide. Plants of the bull kelp (*Durvillea antarctica*) torn by the waves from nearby rock are washed on to the beach and these provide food for some of the inhabitants.

which removes much of the finer sediment and may in exceptionally bad weather strip the beach down to gravel or even base rock.

Two small crustaceans mark the upper shore. The sandhopper *Talorchestia quoyana* (Figure 108) is brownish grey and flattened from side to side like other amphipods: however, it does stand upright, supporting itself by stretching the long, hind limbs out sideways. As its common name suggests, it leaps, and this it does very well: the body is first flexed then quickly straightened, thrusting the hind limbs and tail against the sand. These same rear appendages are used to clear away the sand as it is pushed aside by the head. *Talorchestia* remains buried during the day, quite deeply if the surface layers dry out; it will not survive for long if exposed to the sun and wind. Just after dusk, and with the tide receding, it emerges to feed on decaying matter on the surface, sometimes foraging as far as the middle of the beach. Sandhoppers retreat up the beach ahead of the returning tide and burrow back into the sand at dawn. The activity of these animals is very rhythmical and follows the tidal cycle very closely: this rhythm (controlled internally) can be altered by changes in light and temperature. Sandhoppers can orientate themselves on the beach by using a prominent object such as a boulder. *Scyphax ornatus*, a sea slater, is the other species (Figure 109); like other isopods it is flattened from back to belly. The head bears a pair of distinctly elbowed feelers and crescentic eyes; the body is grey and

108. *Talorchestia quoyana*, the sandhopper, is common along the strandline, particularly in places where there is much washed up seaweed (there may be as many as 100 sandhoppers/square metre). The sandhopper moves about the surface at night; during the day it buries itself in the sand, sometimes up to 30 cm. below (the drier the sand, the deeper it goes). Length up to 14 mm.

110. *Amphidesma ventricosum* or toheroa, that much relished table delicacy: it is an inhabitant of surf pounded sand beaches, particularly those along the western coast of the North Island. Often numerous (up to 60/m²), the adults congregate to form distinct beds on the middle shore, and the young are widely scattered. Small and middle sized toheroas are eaten, at high tide, by the snapper (*Chrysophrys auratus*) and, at low tide, by the red-billed gull (*Larus scopulinus*). The animal photographed is lying on its side protruding its foot (at the rounded front end of the shell) and two breathing tubes or siphons (at the angular hind end). Length (of the shell) up to 11 cm.

111. *Amphidesma subtriangulatum*, the tuatua, is the dominant shellfish of sandy beaches at many places around the coast. It lives at a lower level on the beach and is more numerous (up to 20/m².) than the adult toheroa. Length (of the shell) up to 7 cm.

the plates of the back have a finely granular texture. During the day *Scyphax* remains in its burrow, a deep vertical shaft: at night when the sand is still damp after the ebbing tide, it emerges to join *Talorchestia* in its search for rotting plant and animal remains.

Dominating the middle shore are species from two different groups of animals. Crustacea are as supreme here as they are on the upper and lower beach zones: here they are isopods, smaller and not so easy to identify as *Scyphax* and are therefore best noted and left. Clams are the other group. Two species, both very well known to the general public, are characteristic of the sandy beach: they are the toheroa, *Amphidesma ventricosum*, and the tuatua, *Amphidesma subtriangulatum*; they are seldom found together. The toheroa (Figure 110) lives on the very exposed beaches of the west coast of the North Island and at the southern tip of the South Island. The shell, white marked with yellow and black, is elliptical in outline except for the bump at the hinge and, although fairly substantial, shatters easily: it is fairly narrow when the two valves are closed together. The flesh is cream in colour but appears pale yellow when contracted. The toheroa lives up to one foot down and can dig very rapidly for a bivalved shellfish. During the open season lay one of your catch on the surface of the beach and see how quickly it disappears below. The large tongue-like foot, almost half the size of the body when fully extended, is thrust out between the valves of the shell, and stuck into the sand; when the foot is fixed by enlargement at the tip, the shell is raised vertically. The foot, now below the surface, is extended and fixed again and the shell drawn down – this is repeated until the whole animal is completely buried. At the bottom of its burrow the toheroa maintains contact with the surface when the tide is in; two long tubes (siphons) are extended from the rear of the shell to the entrance of the burrow. Water is drawn in through one of these, tested first by the fringe of tiny sensory processes at the opening (a large or noxious particle, or water of a different temperature or salinity can be excluded by the animal closing and withdrawing its siphons). As in bivalves such as the mussel, oyster or piddock water is pumped through for respiration and feeding; as the water passes through the gills oxygen and carbon dioxide are exchanged and little plants and fine organic particles removed for food. Used water is expelled through the other siphon (the one nearest the hinge).

On other sandy beaches the tuatua (Figure 111) replaces the toheroa. However, they do not have the same distribution across the beach, the tuatua extends to a lower level and here its population is densest. The shell is like that of the toheroa except it is very angular at the hinge (hence the second name *subtriangulatum*). The siphons are shorter, but this is not very surprising since the tuatua burrows only shallowly. Otherwise it lives in a similar manner to the toheroa.

The lower shore is difficult to sample; you will have to wait for a calm period before attempting to do so. Small crustacea, this time amphipods, are very characteristic of this zone of the beach. There are, however, several different species and none is easy to recognize from a photograph; for this reason we have ignored them. A common, much bigger, crustacean is also an excellent indicator of the lower shore; it is the common swimming crab, *Ovalipes catharus* (Figure 112). It is hard to spot when swimming since its body and limbs are sand coloured, but once captured it is easy to identify. The rim of the front half of the body is sharply toothed and the tips of the last pair of legs are paddle-shaped. Identification is clinched by the two prominent mauve spots near the back end of the body. Like some of the crabs of the rocky shore, this one is rather pugnacious when cornered and the slender but strong and sharply toothed nippers can inflict a painful wound. *Ovalipes* swims about looking for food – it is a scavenger like many other crabs. Swimming is produced by powerful strokes of the paddles; these same limbs are also used to dig out the sand as the animal buries itself, back end first

---

50. Fauna of an overhang (the roof of a small cave) in the lower shore zone on a basalt reef (East coast of the North Island). The front-rear axis of the overhang is the diagonal running from the top right to bottom left corner. At the top right corner is the sea-mat *Dakaria subovoidea* (better known as *Watersipora cucullata*), a thin, brittle, black crust edged with orange: this sea-mat also grows on open rock, wharf piles and the hulls of boats — it is now a very common fouling organism in the Auckland Harbour (probably brought by ships from Australia). Dot-like yellow bodies of the boring sponge *Cliona celata* relieve the black of the sea-mat. Next to the black sea-mat is a distinct zone of *Tethya aurantium*, the golf ball sponge. Much of the rest of this overhang is covered by the sponges *Suberites axellinoides* (dull orange) and *Microciona coccinea* (bright red). Several patches of the very characteristic overhang sponge *Ircinia fasiculata* (dark grey, thick with cone-like projections) are present at the left side near the bottom and amongst the golf ball sponges on the right. About a quarter of the way down the left side are two simple sea-squirts, *Asterocarpa coerulea* (cream and blue) and *Pyura rugata* (reddish brown). The two brown banded snail shells are the lined whelk (*Buccinulum lineum*).

51. *Tethya aurantium*, the yellow or orange golf ball sponge, is widespread and very common in occurrence and favours dampish, shaded positions. Large groups live on the under surfaces of ledges, roofs and floors of small caves and on the sides of deep rock pools on the lower half of the shore. Diameter up to 6 cm.

88

45. *Tripterygium robustum*, a cockabully which lives in pools and under stones on silty harbour reefs. The male (see photograph) is distinguished from the female by the darker colouration and the pale yellow crescent-shaped marking at the base of the pectoral (first) fins. During the breeding season the male establishes a territory (a small area of the shore) which it defends against other males: a male may breed with several females and guards the eggs until they hatch. Length up to 9 cm.

47. *Siphonaria zelandica*, a siphon shell (a pulmonate limpet), is a common inhabitant of shallow pools, runnels and crevices on the upper half of the middle shore on sheltered parts of the exposed coast; although limpet-shaped, *Siphonaria* has not the adhesive power of a true limpet. A herbivore, it shows little selectivity taking all seaweeds growing in its zone; *Enteromorpha intestinalis*, *Chaetomorpha linum* and *Ulva* are prominent in its diet. *Siphonaria* dislikes being continually covered or uncovered by the sea; it can withstand a considerable loss of water and large changes in salinity. As an individual grows it establishes a 'home' (as in the true limpets, a scar on the rock into which the shell fits snugly), a point of safety from which it forages (this it does for several hours after being uncovered by the tide). Length up to 25 mm.

Figure 50   See facing page

Figure 51   See facing page

Figure 52
See facing page

Figure 53   See facing page

Figure 54   See facing page

Figure 55   See facing page

Figure 56   See facing page

(it retains contact with the sea by protruding its feelers out of the narrow opening of the burrow.

The strandline is littered, particularly after a storm, with all sorts of shells, mainly of the bivalve type. Some of these do live on the beach at extreme low water, but most come from beyond. We need say little else about them here; they are very difficult to collect alive and not much is known about their habits.

MUD

The mudflat (Figure 113) is the least appealing part of the shore to search for sea life. Mud smells, and it splatters your clothes and tires you out by clinging to your feet as you walk, or should we say stagger, across it. Most mudflats are wide and it is a long, exhausting trek to the edge of the sea at low tide. Digging and sifting mud is hard work too and you need plenty of water to wash just one clod through the sieve; it pays therefore to follow the sea, in or out, as you explore the flat.

---

52. *Actinothoe albocincta.* This sea-anemone is quite variable in colour; sometimes the stripes are pink and white, brown and yellow, or pale green and orange brown. It often lives in groups in rock pools, under ledges and on wharf piles at low tide mark in harbour waters. Including the tentacles, up to 4 cm. across.

53. *Diadumene neozelanica,* quite a wide-ranging sea-anemone since it lives on both the open coast, on mussels, and in harbours, near low tide mark under ledges, in piddock burrows and on wharf piles. Unlike most other sea-anemones, *Diadumene* feeds on tiny animals of the plankton; for this reason it is not a suitable animal for the home aquarium. Including the tentacles, up to 6 cm. across.

54. *Actinia tenebrosa,* the sea-waratah or red beadlet. Best known of the local sea-anemones, it is numerous on the upper half of the middle shore on the lower surface of an overhang, on the shaded sides of smooth boulders and in caves in places where the water is fairly clear. Including the tentacles, up to 7 cm. across.

55. *Microcosmus kura.* This sea-squirt lives, often in large clumps, on the underside of overhanging ledges, on silted rock and wharf piles near low water in harbours. *Microcosmus* is only recorded for the eastern coast of the northern finger of the North Island. Length up to 48 mm.

56. *Asterocarpa coerulea,* a sea-squirt which lives near low tide mark on the under surface of overhangs and on the sides of both loose and fixed rocks on fairly sheltered areas of the open coast and in harbours where there is not a thick layer of silt. Northern finger of the North Island from the Hokianga Harbour to the Hauraki Gulf. Length up to 43 mm.

As a habitat the mudflat is quite the opposite of the sandy beach; it is wide, nearly flat and very soft. The swash and backwash of the gentle waves have the same force and the deposit is therefore laid down evenly; there is no great accumulation of large particles at the top of the beach. The average particle size is small; in harbours and estuaries, where water movement is very slight, very fine particles settle. In such quiet waters the deposit is not shifted about and this, of course, makes the mudflat very suitable for animals which build permanent homes. The deposit is flooded with water and there may even be areas of standing water at low tide; drying out is never a problem. The spaces between

113. A small part of a mudflat. Some of the large harbours, such as the Manukau (where this photograph was taken) have very extensive areas of intertidal mud, some up to six or seven miles wide (the mudflat in the foreground is over one mile across).

the particles are small and therefore the circulation of water (and oxygen) is poor. Organic matter is plentiful and it may form as much as one-twentieth of the flat. As a result of poor oxygenation and high organic content the black layer almost reaches the surface. Lack of oxygen is overcome, however, by the animals having their burrows opening at the surface and drawing down water from above. The wall of a burrow is much lighter in colour than the rest of the sediment; oxygen in the water circulating through the burrow breaks down the black iron sulphide. Deposit feeding is much practised because of the high organic content. Digging is easy as most of the particles are small and, because of its flooded condition, the deposit becomes very fluid with agitation. Animals like fan worms which collect food with delicate feathery processes are noticeably absent; large quantities of fine particles interfere with the proper functioning of the feeding (and breathing) apparatus. Since the deposit is very stable large plants can occupy the flat.

Mudflats do change in shape and detail with time; the main agent here is freshwater run-off, either as seepage from the adjacent land or as the main body of the river, changing course and refashioning the channels and flats. It is still possible to distinguish the three main shore zones, marked not by any physical features of the deposit but by the organisms.

The lower shore is identified by two crustaceans. One of them is a snapping shrimp, *Alpheus* sp. (a species still to be named). *Alpheus* (Figure 114) is about the size of the common prawn but of slightly heavier build; the suit of plates is transparent, highly polished and marked with fawn, and the bluish green digestive gland shows through at the front end. The first pair of nippers are greatly enlarged, one of the pair being much bigger than the other. It makes its own burrow, a system of twisting, sometimes branching, tunnels connecting with the surface by oblique or vertical shafts. A snapping shrimp is an easy animal to locate for, like the cicada or cricket, it identifies its position by making a recognizable sound. As you walk across the lower beach you will hear this noise which is rather like the ragged volleying of cap pistols. What actually happens is that the shrimp cocks the movable finger of its nipper, like the hammer of a pistol; it is then released (triggered) and a peg on the finger is thrust into a socket (in the large segment of the claw) forcing water out and creating the sound. You may wonder what the snapping sound is for. We guess that it is a signal to others of the species, but whether it serves to keep them together (to form a well-knit group or population) or apart (to frighten a hopeful squatter away from the burrow or space out the individuals of a population), or is part of the reproductive ceremony, we cannot say. This snapping shrimp swims well, but when the tide is in it spends much of its time either lurking just inside its burrow waiting for a dainty morsel to go walking, by, or creeping about the surface searching for dead or dying animals. A mantis shrimp, *Lysiosquilla spinosa* (Figure 115), is the other species. At first sight this crustacean looks like a member of the shrimp-prawn group, but it is not. It belongs to a very special group, standing well apart from the shrimps and prawns. *Lysiosquilla spinosa* is easy to

---

57. A crevice in the middle shore zone (lower part) of a basalt reef. A piece of rock has been removed to show the sediment which has collected in the crevice making it a special habitat: the outer region of the crevice, free of debris, is indicated by the black sea-mat *Dakaria subovoidea* (penetrating inside from the open rock), the middle region by the pieces of broken shell and the inner region by the fine sediment. The inhabitants of this particular crevice were *Timarete anchylochaeta, Terebella haplochaeta* and *Dendrostomum aeneum* in the inner region, and *Marphysa depressa, Perinereis novaehollandiae* and *Amphiporus* sp. in the middle region. The open rock is heavily covered with the black sea-mat *Dakaria subovoidea* (= *Watersipora cucullata*), the calcareous red seaweed *Corallina officinalis* (pink and fawn patches) and the green seaweed *Codium adhaerens* (two dark green patches).

58. *Isactinia olivacea*, the olive beadlet or olive green sea-anemone, is not always green — sometimes it is khaki or red brown. Sometimes it attaches small pieces of shell to its body. In pools, large and small, it extends to the upper edge of the middle shore; it also lives in damp crevices, small pits, and in old piddock burrows. Including the tentacles, up to 7 cm. across.

59. *Eulalia microphylla*, a bristle worm. A common worm, often active when the rock is fairly dry, living amongst barnacles and the tube worm *Pomatoceros* as well as in crevices. Young ragworms (a common species is *Perinereis novaehollandiae*) form part of its diet. Length up to 23 cm.

60. *Perinereis novaehollandiae*, the common ragworm or, as it is sometimes called, the green sea-centipede. This bristle worm (centipede is a misnomer), probably the best known of its kind in New Zealand, has a wide distribution down the rocky shore: it lives in crevices, under loose rocks, in kelp holdfasts, empty piddock burrows, amongst mussels, rock oysters and the tube worm *Pomatoceros*. Small individuals are pale in colour. Length up to 40 cm.

61. *Onchidella nigricans*, one of the few seashore relatives of the land snails (*Siphonaria* is another). It lives throughout the middle shore and is active on open rock whenever it is damp; at other times it hides in crevices, or between rock oysters or other sessile animals. *Onchidella*, like the black nerite (*Nerita melanotragus*), occurs in groups which reassemble after each feeding excursion. Length up to 23 mm.

Figure 57   See facing page

Figure 58   See facing page

Figure 59   See facing page

Figure 60   See facing page

Figure 61   See facing page

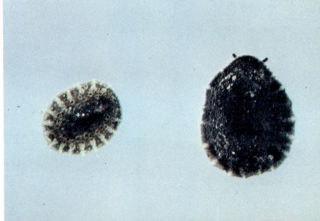

62. *Amphiporus* sp., a ribbon or proboscis worm. A common inhabitant of the lower part of the middle shore on harbour reefs, it is often to be seen part way out of a crevice or empty piddock burrow searching the still damp open rock for living prey. Length up to 105 mm.

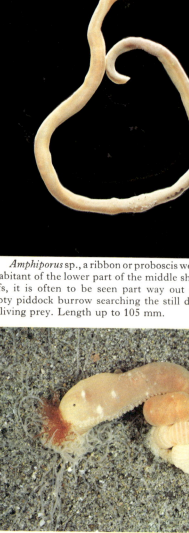

63. *Timarete anchylochaeta*, a bristle worm, is common, on the lower half of the shore, in sediment in crevices, empty piddock burrows and beneath loose rocks. Length up to 5 cm.

64. *Terebella haplochaeta*, a bristle worm, which is very common in the same habitats as *Timarete*; it also lives in the *Corallina* turf and kelp holdfasts. Length up to 6 cm.

70. *Stylarioides parmatus*, a bristle worm, bores into soft rock in the lower part of the piddock zone (in the photograph the rock is broken to show the reflected attitude assumed by the animal in its burrow). Only occasional in occurrence. Length up to 6 cm.

Figure 64
Figure 70

71. *Marphysa depressa*, a bristle worm sometimes called a rockworm, is a fairly common middle shore inhabitant of more sheltered reefs; it forms a fairly tightly fitting burrow in soft rock and fine sediment lodged in old piddock burrows and crevices. Small individuals can often be found living in the mud of the eelgrass (*Zostera nana*) bed. Length up to 35 cm.

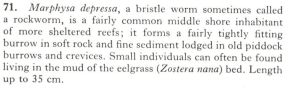

Figure 72   See next text page

Figure 73   See next text page

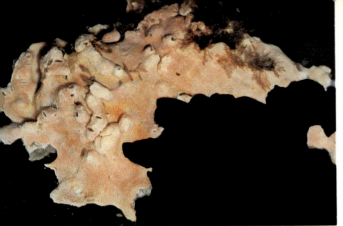

Figure 74   See facing page

Figure 75   See facing page

Figure 76   See facing page

Figure 77   See facing page

Figure 78   See facing page

Captions for colour plates   72, 73, 74, 75, 76, 77, 78

72.   Loose rocks, some up to 1 m. across, covering a mudstone platform on a moderately protected part of the open (East) coast; these rocks are uncovered more than this on an extreme spring tide. The abundant brown seaweed is *Carpophyllum plumosum*. The fauna living under these rocks is diverse, abundant and very colourful.

73.   The under surface of one of the smaller rocks (about 0·3 m. across) shown in Figure 72. The principal animals, all permanently attached (the mobile animals having escaped), are: the sea-squirt *Corella eumyota* (large, purplish pink, oval body with obvious opening, the atrial siphon, at the top right corner of the rock), the sea-squirt *Asterocarpa cerea* (much smaller than *Corella*, cream or brownish elliptical bodies, each with a pair of openings (the siphons), mostly on the left half of the rock), the calcareous sponge *Leucosolenia* sp. (yellow network just to the right of the centre line), the bristle worm *Spirorbis borealis* (little white tightly coiled tubes scattered over the left half of the rock), the empty tubes of several other bristle worms, and several species of sea-mat (the crusty looking patches, each a colony, of various colours and sizes, completely covering the rock on the right and only partly on the left).

74.   *Didemnum candidum*, a colonial or compound sea-squirt, is quite common in harbours and on moderately sheltered places on the open coast growing on the under surfaces of rocks, on seaweeds such as *Hormosira banksii* and *Cystophora torulosa*, and on wharf piles. Colony up to 18 cm. across (grows as a very thin crust on hard surfaces and a thick one on soft surfaces).

75.   *Galeolaria hystrix*, a bristle worm. One of the largest of its kind locally, it is quickly recognized by the prickly stopper, and white and red tube. *Galeolaria* is common on the lower shore in fairly clear waters, on the under surfaces of loose rocks, the sides of caves and on kelp holdfasts. The specimen in the photograph has protruded its feathery tentacles for feeding and breathing. Length up to 25 mm.

76.   *Rynella impacta*, the nesting mussel. A single specimen with its 'blanket' removed; the anchoring threads (byssus) are visible jutting from the opening of the shell. *Rynella* often occurs in small groups, their 'blankets' woven together to form a 'nest': it is fairly common on kelp holdfasts and the under surfaces or rocks on the lower shore. Length (of the shell) up to 42 mm.

77.   *Dendrodoris citrina*, a dorid sea-slug which is common in harbours and less so on the open coast. At low tide it can be found under rocks and overhangs, in crevices, on the *Corallina* turf, and crawling across the bottom or even floating upside down at the surface film in places where there is standing water. It varies in colour from very pale yellow to deep orange, and individuals of the open coast may be mottled with brown. Length up to 75 mm.

78.   *Pleurobranchaea novaezelandiae*, a side-gilled sea-slug which is quite common under rocks on sheltered parts of the open coast. Length up to 9 cm.

recognize: it is rather flattened back to belly with some of the plates ridged and spiny; the shield (carapace) which covers the front part of the body is short and does not completely cover the region of the walking legs as it does in the true shrimps. What clinches the identity of this animal is the second pair of legs which, at rest, are held flexed like the first legs of the praying mantis, an insect, and are used in exactly the same way. Both insect and crustacean are carnivorous; these limbs are extended and the spiny business end opened, then withdrawn and closed on the unfortunate prey. Snapping shrimps are often attacked and occasionally one may be cut clean in half with a single stroke of the claws. The mantis shrimp swims more steadily than a prawn and is a better acrobat. Its highly flexible body enables it to turn, somersault and loop tightly and it can do all this inside its burrow, a deep, vertical shaft with a neat, round opening.

The middle shore is very wide and is indicated by another crustacean, *Hemiplax hirtipes*, the stalk-eyed mud crab (Figure 116). The body is rectangular, sharply toothed at the front corners and indented at the back. The legs are long, fairly slender and hairy, and the tips curve and taper to a very fine point: the nippers are long and slender. Background colour of the body is greyish green to reddish brown and imposed on this is a delicate or heavy pattern of dark purple spots: the legs are the same colour, sometimes lighter. This crab defends its burrow, which it either makes itself or borrows from another animal, against others of its kind. The owner or occupant as the case may be, threatens an intruder by posing with the legs spread widely and the nippers drooping.

116. *Hemiplax hirtipes*, the stalk-eyed mud crab, is of the same crab family as the swift running ghost crab of tropical beaches and nipper waving (male only) fiddler crabs of tropical mudflats and temperate sand beaches and salt marshes. *Hemiplax* inhabits flats and eel-grass beds, and the outer zone of salt marshes. Width of the body up to 18 mm.

117. *Chione stutchburyi*, the cockle or tuangi: the animal in the photograph is open with the fringed entrance and exit siphons (for the breathing-respiratory current) extended. The cockle often dominates (sometimes up to 1000/m.²) mudflats of harbours and estuaries; also, with the pipi, it occurs on beaches of muddy sand. The largest individuals live beyond the flat in shallow water; their large size seems to be the result of longer feeding time. Length (of the shell) up to 52 mm.

If the intruder stands its ground, then the owner of the burrow holds its nippers outstretched and pushes the intruder away from the entrance, continuing to do so until the latter yields and retreats, usually unharmed. Only the males fight and at the height of the breeding season groups of them may be observed brawling, for no apparent reason. *Hemiplax* emerges to feed on the surface whether the tide is out or in; it eats carrion or organic matter in the deposit which it digs up with its nippers and sorts with its mouthparts.

Clams also mark the middle shore zone. The lower half of this zone is dominated by the cockle or tuangi, *Chione stutchburyi* (Figure 117); this species may be so abundant that the animals are packed together tightly in their bed, much to the delight of such sea birds as the South Island pied oyster catchers (*Haematopus ostralegus finschi*) and godwit (*Limosa lapponica*). The cockle has a somewhat globular shell with the apex bent towards the front end and with prominent ribs down and across the valves though this sculpture may be very worn in old individuals. Young shells are white, but older ones are marked with reddish brown, particularly at the front end, and purple where the surface is worn. The flesh inside is dirty white except for the siphons (breathing tubes) which are striped with dark grey and the tiny tentacles finely hooped with grey and yellow. A shallow burrower, the cockle leaves the back end protruding through the surface: the siphons are short and the water drawn in is monitored with the tentacles, as in other suspension feeders. Cockles are fairly mobile for a bivalve mollusc; the long foot is used not only to pull the animal into the deposit but also along the surface for short distances. Keeping the cockle company at the surface, particularly higher up the middle shore, is a small bivalve, a nut shell,

119. *Macomona liliana*, the hanikura or large wedge shell, a common inhabitant of mud flats, eel-grass beds and muddy sand beaches; it lives evenly spaced and deeply buried, reaching the surface with the long, thin siphons (partly extended in the photograph). Length (of the shell) up to 55 mm.

120. *Cyclomactra ovata*, a trough shell. Like *Macomona*, with which it occurs though it is not as common, *Cyclomactra* is a deep burrower. The animal in the photograph has protruded its foot and fused siphons (with dark tips), both only partially, and the edge of the cloak or mantle (secretes the shell). Length (of the shell) up to 85 mm.

Figure 79

81. *Odontosyllis polycera*, a bristle worm of clear waters occurring beneath rocks and boulders which do not dry out when uncovered by the tide: it is not common. Length up to 35 mm.

80. *Lamellaria ophione*, a sea snail with an internal shell which feeds on colonial sea-squirts such as *Didemnum psammatodes* (a close relative of *Didemnum candidum*). This snail inhabits the under surfaces of loose rocks on the lower shore, gripping the surface tightly; when dislodged, it curls up and produces a lot of sticky mucus containing an acid secretion (its defence). Occasional only, in the sheltered waters along the North Island coast. Length up to 18 mm.

79. *Phidiana militaris*, an aeolid sea-slug which lives and feeds on sea-firs (hydroids) growing on the under surface of loose rocks on the lower shore in sheltered places, or in pools, on wharf piles or on the green mussel, sometimes to mean tidal level. This sea-slug is cannibalistic when kept without hydroid food. *Phidiana militaris* is found northwards from Banks Peninsula. Length up to 42 mm.

83. *Thysanozoon brochii*, a polyclad flatworm called the skirt dancer. Though usually met with on the under surfaces of low tidal rocks, it may sometimes be seen swimming amongst seaweeds. It is fairly rare and is restricted to the east coast of northern North Island. Length up to 32 mm.

82. *Lepidonotus polychroma*, a scale worm, is common to mean tidal level on most reefs where it inhabits crevices, the holdfasts of large seaweeds, and the spaces between and empty tubes or shells of such zoning animals as *Pomatoceros, Sabellaria* and *Xenostrobus*. Length up to 2 cm.

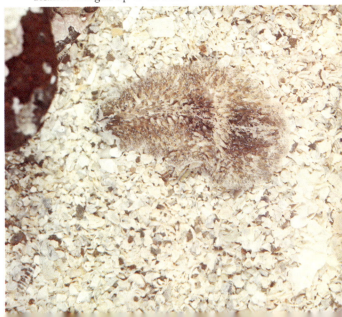

84. *Buccinulum heteromorphum*, a small whelk which is not uncommon under stones on the lower shore; a North Island species, occurring from the Bay of Plenty northwards on the east coast and in the Manukau Harbour on the west. The specimen in the photograph shows the usual shell pattern; sometimes individuals are encountered which either have very even lines on the shell (no blotches of colour) or the shell is plain. Height (of the shell) up to 19 mm.

85. *Patiriella regularis*, the common cushion star, is one of our commonest starfish. An inhabitant of the lower shore, it lives on open rock, under ledges or rocks. Bluish green is the commonest colour of this starfish, but sometimes you will see individuals which are black, orange or red. *Patiriella* feeds mainly on small barnacles, encrusting seaweeds and fine organic debris (which it entangles in mucus); occasionally it eats larger prey such as sea snails and the half crab *Petrolisthes elongatus*. Arm-spread up to 6 cm.

86. *Stegnaster inflatus*, a cushion star. A lower shore species, it particularly favours reefs in clear waters. Infrequent in occurrence, it is found from Banks Peninsula northwards. This cushion star feeds on small crabs, the cat's eye and dead fish. Arm-spread up to 9 cm.

87. *Acanthoclinus quadridactylus*, the rock fish, lives on shores of loose rock, particularly in harbours. Although the rockfish eats a wide variety of small shore animals, some of these, such as the half crab and amphipods, form the bulk of its diet; this seems to be the result of their commonness and not that they are preferred food. A male fish, probably the male parent, guards, and possibly fans, the eggs (bound in a large, round mass) whilst they develop. Length up to 20 cm.

Nucula hartvigiana (Figure 118). The shell is bluntly triangular in shape, polished, and yellowish green marked with brown. Its burrow, a shallow pit, is only a temporary home for it moves about quite a lot at the surface. The foot, although used like other bivalves, has a fairly broad, flat tip; this sole has two halves which are opened for fixation and closed for forcing through the deposit. Unlike most other bivalves, *Nucula* feeds on organic particles within the sediment, collecting and sorting them with a pair of large folded processes (palps) which flank the mouth. The small gills are purely respiratory and there are no breathing tubes; water enters at the head end, passes through the gill plates and leaves at the rear.

Of the clams the surface dwellers do not have sole right to the middle shore, for deep below live two common species, *Macomona liliana*, a tellin called locally the hanikura, and *Cyclomactra ovata*, a trough shell. *Macomona* (Figure 119) occurs over much of this zone and is only replaced near the top by *Cyclomactra*. The white shell is thin, flat and roughly oval in outline: at the posterior (narrower) end the valves are bent to the right (upwards in life since the animal lies on its left side) and through this little culvert the breathing tubes are directed upwards. Long and slender when extended, the translucent white breathing tubes are mobile: the lower one (the inlet pipe) is used like the nozzle of a vacuum cleaner to suck up the fine sediment which is deposited on the surface of the beach with each tide; the lower tube is the outlet. The position of an animal can be easily identified by marks on the surface of the beach; the sucking of the inlet siphon leaves a group of radiating channels which look like the foot-print of a bird. *Cyclomactra* (Figure 120) is a much bigger and heavier built bivalve. The shell is elliptical in outline except for the prominent beak at the hinge, thick but fractures

122. *Zeacumantus lutulentus,* the large horn shell (a cerith or creeper), is a very common inhabitant of flats and muddy reefs in harbours and estuaries north of Banks Peninsula. It ploughs its way across the surface mud leaving a recognizable trail (sometimes its jelly-like spawn string is encountered). One of the animals photographed is showing its foot, tentacles and snout. Height (of the shell) up to 30 mm.

easily, and dirty white stained with black near the lower edge. Lying deep in its burrow, *Cyclomactra* makes contact with the surface through its breathing tubes which are long and fused, and translucent white except for the grey pigment between the short sensory processes at the tip. It feeds on minute organisms and detritus floating in the water when the sea covers the beach.

Three snails are common inhabitants of the surface of the middle shore: they are the whelk *Cominella glandiformis*, the cerith or creeper *Zeacumantus lutulentus* and the top shell *Zediloma subrostrata*. *Cominella* (Figure 121) is an active carnivore and scavenger, moving about easily

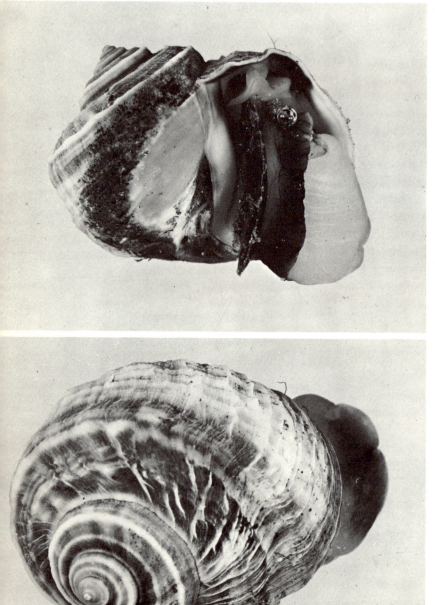

124. *Amphibola crenata*, the mud snail or titiko, is common on mud, particularly in mangrove swamps and the seaward side of salt-marshes. Though it favours exposed wet mud, the mud snail is quite tolerant of permanent submergence in fresh water (will survive in it for about one week) and salt water (for two or three weeks). *Amphibola* buries itself during the flood tide, emerging on the ebb to feed on the surface mud. The collar-shaped spawn, eggs compacted with mud, is very distinctive and is often seen at the side of a trail. The bottom photograph is a view from above with the head poking out beyond the aperture: the top is a side view with the animal partly retracted; the fleshy foot folded, bearing the operculum, fills most of the aperture of the shell; the opening of the 'lung', with lips, is to the top of the aperture. Height (of the shell) up to 25 mm.

and quickly over the surface looking for living *Chione* or dead animals. The shell is a low spire, regularly knobbed, bluish or greenish grey, faintly banded and the body whorl sometimes white (though the outside colour is masked by a thin film of mud), and purple or purplish brown inside. The animal is white densely marked with black on the sides and upper parts and on the long breathing tube, which protrudes from the anterior canal of the shell, and around the eyes situated on the short tentacles: the oval stopper or operculum is black and brown. Singly or in groups this whelk attacks living cockles by inserting the narrow proboscis through a gap in the prey's shell (where the valves of the cockle's shell do not fit exactly) and tearing at the flesh with the spiny tongue. *Zeacumantus lutulentus* (Figure 122) differs from *Z. subcarinatus*, an inhabitant of high level rock pools, in having a taller shell; the colour of the body is the same. This species is a deposit feeder, passing huge quantities of mud through its gut to extract the contained organic matter. *Zediloma subrostrata* (Figure 123) lives mainly where there is a firm surface such as a large piece of broken shell, a stone or even an old car tyre, feeding on the film of mud and small plants which it scrapes up with its horny tongue. This top shell is greenish yellow with oblique stripes of black. The ground colour of the soft parts is yellowish green which is very dark on the snout; there is a dense covering of black pigment on the top of the head, along the sides of the body just beneath the frill, on the eye stalks and flaps, and a little on the long head and body tentacles.

Two animals, both easy to recognize, are good indicators of the upper shore; one is the mud snail, *Amphibola crenata*, the other is the tunnelling mud crab, *Helice crassa*. *Amphibola* (Figure 124), like *Onchidella* and *Siphonaria*, is a relative of the land snails and slugs; however, its kinship

125. *Helice crassa*, the tunnelling mud crab, is swift running and nimble; it is very alert too, for it responds to a movement up to 50 metres away, usually by retreating into its burrow. On the upper shore *Helice* (up to 50/m.²) replaces *Hemiplax* as the dominant crab of muddy beaches: *Helice* is very tolerant of fresh water and penetrates far into estuaries. Width of the body up to 13 mm.

is fairly distant since it still retains, as do many marine snails, an operculum (thin, curved with a jagged outer edge, transparent, reddish brown) and a larval stage. The shell is plump with a very low spire and in large individuals wrinkled rather like a walnut: the outer surface is dull yellowish brown with darker brown patches, the inner is glossy, purplish brown or brown. The animal has a broad foot for crawling across soft mud: there are no tentacles, instead there is a sensory groove close to each eye, and the opening of the respiratory chamber or 'lung' (*Amphibola* breathes air) is guarded by a pair of lips, a small outer and a large, frilly inner one. *Amphibola* feeds by eating the deposit for the contained organic matter; the long faecal strings laid on the surface of the mudflat indicate the enormous amount of mud which the animal swallows to obtain nutriment. The other species, *Helice crassa* (Figure 125), extends higher than *Amphibola*, reaching to the inner edge of the salt marsh which on the mudflat is the upper limit of the shore; the lower limit for *Helice* is on the middle shore. There is no need to dig for this crab, just stand or squat quietly and soon they emerge from their burrows to stand motionless and watch; a sudden movement by you and they quickly retreat. *Helice* looks rather like *Hemiplax*, but can be distinguished by the nearly square body, and shorter nippers and eyestalks (the length of the eyestalk is much less than the distance between the two eyes). The body is olive green to brownish yellow and the pincers are yellow with yellowish brown along the upper edge. This crab seems to spend most of its life making, mending and defending its burrow, a short, curved shaft, sometimes with two openings. Moving in and out of its burrow sideways, it kicks up the mud with the walking legs, pushing out the excavated deposit with the trailing set. Unlike *Hemiplax, Helice* is only active when the tide is out; by recirculating the little water lying on the surface through the respiratory chambers it is able to keep its gills moist. However, food and feeding behaviour are very similar, so is the defence of territory. The threatening attitude of *Helice* differs in that a tiptoe stance is adopted and the nippers are held aloft and open, both sexes do it and it is not maintained for so long. Also, individuals gang up and raid the burrow of another; real blows are exchanged during the ensuing skuffle.

In our introduction to beaches, we mentioned that most large plants are excluded because of the instability of the deposit. However, in the quietest areas of harbours and estuaries a few species of large plants occupy much of the mudflat and are a very distinctive feature. Throughout New Zealand the very top of the mudflat is turned into marsh by

100

126. The mangrove (*Avicennia resinifera*): a small tree (the mangrove grows to a height of 8 m. in the harbours of northern North Island) is shown standing in an open area of the swamp, its 'breathing' roots poking through the surface of the surrounding mud which is very fine in texture, waterlogged and oxygenated only to a very little depth. The trunk and 'breathing' roots offer a firm surface for sedentary animals and trees on the seaward side of the swamp and along the channels are colonized by the rock oyster (*Crassostrea glomerata*), the little black mussel (*Xenostrobus pulex*) and the barnacle *Elminius modestus*. Common inhabitants of swamp mud are the mud snail (*Amphibola crenata*), the large horn shell (*Zeacumantus lutulentus*), the whelk (*Cominella glandiformis*), the tunnelling mud crab (*Helice crassa*) and the snapping shrimp (*Alpheus* sp.), the last two make burrows.

such flowering plants as the glasswort, *Salicornia australis*, the sea rush, *Juncus maritimus*, and the jointed rush, *Leptocarpus simplex*, which can cope with a salty soil. In the south the glasswort flourishes, forming

101

a wide lush seaward zone to the marsh: it is present in the north but is not very successful and this zone is narrow, sparse and patchy. The inner or upper part of the marsh is marked by the two rushes; only the jointed rush occurs throughout the country, the sea rush petering out in the southern half of the South Island. The sea may penetrate the upper part of the marsh through channels.

Along the coasts of the Auckland Province the boundary between the upper and middle shore zones is turned into a swamp by the mangrove or manawa (Figure 126) – a touch of tropical climes. A substantial tree when fully grown; the bark is grey and the oval leaves are deep green and glossy above and greyish yellow and matt below. Northwards the mangrove swamps increase in extent and the individual trees are larger. It is strange to see a land plant doing so well in the sea; it succeeds because it can draw water from the salty environment. This precious water is stored in the leaves; loss by evaporation is reduced by the thick

127. Part of an eel-grass (*Zostera nana*) bed, a distinctive habitat of the mud beach. The important features of the eel-grass habitat are the high organic content and softness of the sediment, and the firm though flexible surfaces for walking or attachment offered by the long, narrow leaves.

128. *Haminoea zelandiae*, a bubble shell, lives on eel-grass beds, particularly where there is standing water. It lays (during winter) a very distinctive spawn; this is a sausage-shaped mass of jelly with a string of small, yellow eggs spirally coiled inside. *Haminoea* is a North Island species. Height (of the shell) up to 22 mm.

129. A muddy sand beach (southern end of Cheltenham Beach, Auckland). In the foreground is a fairly steep, firm bank of sand and fine shell; though such a bank is characteristic of this sort of beach, the nature of the sediment obviously makes it quite a different habitat to the broad, seaward flat of muddy sand by which this beach is identified. Low tide leaves water, from a film to ankle depth, covering large areas of the flat part of the beach.

cuticle. Around the base of the tree pencil-like processes protrude from the mud; these are the aerial roots of the mangrove, very necessary in a 'soil' which lacks oxygen.

The trunk and aerial roots of mangroves on the seaward side of the swamp or along the edge of the deep channels are usually densely covered with the little barnacle *Elminius modestus* – the line where these end is the boundary between the middle and upper shore zones. *Elminius* has four distinctly separate side plates, usually well flattened and white, each bilobed to give the barnacle a star-like appearance: however, in-dividuals living on mangroves are grey, tall and ridged and the charac-teristic shape is lost. It favours shell, wood and metal as a base for settlement and is very tolerant of low salinity (it inhabits estuaries), and cloudy and still water; it is not found in places where there is heavy wave action.

The mangrove, glasswort and rushes are not the only large plants to colonize wide expanses of the mudflat. Where the flat is wide, the water movement still brisk enough to prevent smothering by the finest particles and the saltiness not too low, large beds of eelgrass may be established (Figure 127), stretching from mean tide level to just below extreme low water. As in the mangrove swamp, fine particles collect and make the deposit quite soft. The dark green grass-like plants arise from a creeping root system which binds the deposit and stabilizes the beach. Of the two species occuring locally, *Zostera nana* is the commonest; it can be distinguished by the narrow leaves and open sheaths. Naturally enough, the fauna differs from the bare flat; many of the mudflat species are still present but their numbers and sizes are not the same.

Of the animals which come into their own on the *Zostera* flat, there is space to mention only one. *Haminoea zelandiae*, a bubble shell, is a relative of the sea-slugs described in the chapter on the under rock habitat. Globular, translucent and straw coloured, the shell is much too small to accommodate the fleshy animal (Figure 128). When ex-tended, the body, mottled grey, is streamlined by the head shield and the flaps of skin, outgrowths from the foot, which fold over the shell. It looks a succulent morsel, but is well armed to repel a hopeful diner; when handled the animal discharges an unpleasant secretion from special glands in the gill cavity. At low tide *Haminoea* can be found crawling either on the leaves of *Zostera* or partially embedded in the mud. It is a vegetarian feeding mainly on the delicate green seaweed *Enteromorpha* attached to pieces of shell; the nutritious juices are expressed in the toothed gizzard, a special chamber of the fore-gut.

104

88. *Alope spinifrons*, a prawn. This species is quite common on, and characteristic of, reefs of the open coast. During the day it hides beneath low tidal stones; at night, when the tide is in, it emerges to search the surface of the rock for food. Length up to 75 mm.

89. *Hemigrapsus edwardsi*, the common rock crab. This crab is fairly common under stones on the lower shore in sheltered places: it is moderately tolerant of silt. An aggressive crab, it is not as pugnacious as the related large shore crab, *Leptograpsus variegatus*. The male is quickly identified by the very large nippers and narrow abdomen. Width of the body up to 38 mm.

90. *Cancer novaezelandiae*, the New Zealand cancer crab. Though characteristic of the same shores as *Hemigrapsus edwardsi*, it is not nearly so common. The cancer crab has been reported eating living oysters and mussels, gaining access to the soft insides by breaking the edge of the shell of the prey with its pincers. Width of the body up to 12 cm.

91. *Ozius truncatus*, the black finger crab, is found in the same places as *Cancer novaezelandiae*, and is about as common: it is restricted to the coast of the North Island, being commonest in the north. Width of the body up to 63 mm.

92. *Eurynolambrus australis*, the triangular crab. Perhaps our prettiest shore crab; it favours clear waters, living under loose rocks on the lower shore in places sheltered from heavy waves. Width of the body up to 60 mm.

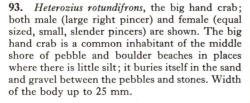

93. *Heterozius rotundifrons*, the big hand crab; both male (large right pincer) and female (equal sized, small, slender pincers) are shown. The big hand crab is a common inhabitant of the middle shore of pebble and boulder beaches in places where there is little silt; it buries itself in the sand and gravel between the pebbles and stones. Width of the body up to 25 mm.

94. *Petrolisthes elongatus*, the common half crab: groups, sometimes several hundred strong, are to be found under stones on the middle shore of reefs on protected parts of the open coast and in harbours. Its main food is fine organic matter, either floating or stirred up from the bottom by the pincers, which is collected by sweeping the water with a pair of large, feathery appendages, right and left used alternately. Width of the body up to 13 mm.

96. *Ischnochiton maorianus*, a coat-of-mail shell or chiton; several colour variations are shown in the photograph. A lower shore species, it lives on the under surfaces of loose stones and rocks on reefs along sheltered parts of the open coast and in harbours. *Ischnochiton* shows little resistance to drying out and fresh water. Although this coat-of-mail shell occurs throughout New Zealand, it is commoner in the north. Length up to 40 mm.

97. *Amaurochiton glaucus*, a coat-of-mail shell. Though about as common as *Ischnochiton maorianus*, this species is much hardier since it inhabits heavily wave washed boulder beaches and the periodically dilute waters of tide pools and inner reaches of harbours, dwelling at a much higher level (the middle shore). *Amaurochiton* is quite variable in colour and pattern, though not producing the spectacular range shown by *Ischnochiton*. Length up to 37 mm.

Figure 98   See facing page

Figure 99   See facing page

Figure 100   See facing page

MUDDY SAND: THE RICHEST BEACH

This is the most popular kind of beach (Figure 129), for the majority of people congregate here to enjoy the sea: the beach is not too muddy and the waves are seldom powerful enough to knock a person over. You will know well enough that the beach is only an attractive playground between high and mid tide, both on the flood and ebb. The top of the beach is fairly short, steep and coarse (a mixture of sand and broken shell), the result of the heavier particles being piled up against the edge of the land (on such beaches the swash is still stronger than the backwash); when covered by the sea this step or bank is a perfect place for swimming. Occasionally this bank will be cut away during a stormy period when the waves become destructive. Seaward of this bank is a wide flat of muddy sand (this is what really concerns us here); so gentle is the slope of this flat that after half tide one has to wade out far to find a depth of water sufficient for swimming. The seaward edge of the bank does not indicate the boundary between the upper and middle shore zones (the faunal divisions employed by us in the previous chapters on beaches); this is high up the steep, coarse bank. However, at this step in the beach there is such a change in the nature of the sediment that the clams, good indicators of the middle shore zone, reach their upper limit here, i.e., well short of the average high tide mark. Some middle shore dwellers,

---

98. (Right) *Notoplax violacea*, a coat-of-mail shell. An uncommon species, usually only one or two are seen on a trip to a shore: characteristic of clear waters, it lives on the under surfaces of rocks on the lower shore. Length up to 50 mm.
(Left) *Cryptoconchus porosus*, the butterfly chiton or karimoan. This chiton or coat-of-mail shell is common on the under surfaces of rocks and overhangs, in moist crevices, and amongst seaweed of the lower shore on reefs in harbours and on the open coast. It feeds on encrusting organisms, preferring sponges and seaweeds. Length up to 65 mm.

99. *Ophiopteris antipodum*, the oar sand star. This brittle-star is a lower shore inhabitant of sheltered reefs of the open coast: it clings to the under surface of large, loose rocks, feeding by catching detritus with strings of mucus as it sweeps the rock with its arms or, occasionally, by browsing on sponges and sea-mats. *Ophiopteris* is not common. Arm-spread up to 18 cm.

100. *Ophionereis fasciata*, the mottled sand star. Like the oar sand star (*Ophiopteris antipodum*), this brittle-star inhabits clear waters; however, it is commoner, extends higher on the shore and feeds principally on plankton. *Ophionereis* lies on, or sometimes slightly buried in, the coarse deposit which collects under loose rocks. Arm-spread up to 14 cm.

such as certain species of bristle worm, are found in this bank, but it must be remembered that the nature of their habitat is much different from that of most of the animals we are considering here. If we move to a more sheltered locality the landward bank is wider, less steep and of a finer grade, and muddy sand inhabitants reach a higher tidal level. On some muddy sand beaches there is a distinct ridge between the part of the flat revealed at neap tides and that at springs; this ridge is a fair guide to the boundary of the lower and middle shore zones.

Muddy sand offers living conditions which are a perfect balance of those at the two extremes, sand and mud (see the preceding chapters). The beach is very wet, for there is standing water (often the neap part of the flat is covered by large shallow pools, held there by the ridge which acts as a dam), there are still sufficient coarse particles to allow adequate circulation of water and oxygen (well enough aerated for animals to live in it without making a proper burrow), the black layer is nearly a foot below the surface (the organic content is not excessive) and the beach is stable enough for the construction of permanent dwellings. The deposit is fairly easy to dig yet it is still firm enough for animals to crawl across the surface. Deposit eating animals are very common for there is ample organic matter in a well oxygenated habitat (they are not confined to a permanent burrow): many of the inhabitants feed on detritus and minute organisms floating in the sea when it covers the beach; fine particles are not too abundant to clog delicate collecting and sorting structures.

The upper shore zone (mainly sand and shell) is indicated by the sand-hopper *Talorchestia quoyana*, though here it is never as common as on the beaches of the open coast. This may be because the deposit is too coarse (dries out quickly and is very difficult to dig in) or that the local authorities keep their beaches clear of washed-up seaweed and animals.

The uppermost part of the middle shore zone is dominated by the pipi, *Amphidesma australe* (Figure 130). The texture and colour of its shell is like that of its close relatives, the toheroa and tuatua, except that it is often stained with light orange brown near the hinge and streaked with black. In shape it is strikingly different in being oblong and having the hinge in the middle of the upper edge (the back): the breathing tubes (siphons) are very short. The soft parts are pale yellow or white except the edge of the cloak of skin (the mantle which secretes the shell) which is grey, and the tips of the breathing tubes which are pink or purple

130. *Amphidesma australe*, the pipi: though a good indicator of muddy sand beaches, it is restricted to areas from mean tidal level down where the deposit is fairly coarse. When the cockle (*Chione stutchburyi*) is present in large numbers on such a beach, increasing the fineness of the deposit with its faeces, the pipi is confined to the bank of coarse material at the back of the beach. The largest pipis are to be found near low tide and in shallow water beyond the shore (the higher growth rate is probably the result of longer feeding time). The pipi is quite tolerant of lowered salinity, penetrating some distance into estuaries. Length (of the shell) up to 6 cm.

picked out with yellow below the rim. The pipi burrows very shallowly leaving the rear end well exposed: it does not seem to object to being completely uncovered as individuals are often encountered lying on their sides at the surface. Like the toheroa and tuatua, the pipi feeds on tiny plants and fine detritus suspended in the sea. Below the pipi the rest of the middle zone is marked by the cockle, *Chione stutchburyi*, here as common as on the mudflat, and *Macomona liliana*, a tellin, which is not quite so abundant.

Several species of bristle worm are prominent at this level: three of these are deposit feeders, all spending much of their working lives passing large amounts of the deposit through the gut for the contained organic matter. *Abarenicola affinis* (Figure 131), a lugworm, is particularly common on some beaches of muddy sand: although it is present throughout the middle zone, greatest numbers (20–30/m²) occur at the level occupied by the pipi. This worm constructs and lives in a U-shaped burrow: one of the limbs of the U, the tail shaft, and the horizontal gallery are open; the other limb, the head shaft, is full of loose deposit which has fallen in from the surface. The two entrances are clearly marked, that of the tail shaft by a long, coiled string of muddy sand (faeces) and the head shaft by a shallow depression. It is a succulent looking worm (one which makes good fish bait): the cylindrical body is divided into two distinct portions of about the same length, the front

107

bearing tree-like gills and swellings carrying the bristles being fatter than the hind part. The colour gradates from yellow at the slender end, the abdomen, through olive to purple at the head; the gills are red with blood. The front end of the gut, the 'throat', when turned out forms a soft, bulbous, papillate proboscis. Clumps of particles are loosened and swallowed as the proboscis is worked rhythmically against the deposit in the head shaft of the burrow. Regions of swelling and constriction continually pass along the body (normally forwards though they can travel either way) these are used for digging, crawling and irrigating the burrow (for respiration). *Abarenicola affinis*, like its European relative *Arenicola marina*, leads a very orderly life. When covered by the tide the cycle of activity is very regular: the animal feeds and irrigates, then creeps backwards to the opening of the tail shaft, defaecates, completing the cycle by moving back to the working face irrigating strongly head-wards as it goes. One cycle takes about forty minutes. At low tide one would expect such activity to either slow down appreciably or cease altogether because of the limited supply of oxygen in the water (in the burrow and surrounds). However, this worm on its tailward excursions traps air with its rear end and bubbles it through the gills. If the oxygen is exhausted then the worm can switch over to an energy source not requiring this gas. Though the pattern of a cycle of activity is never altered, the cycles can be slowed or stopped in adverse conditions. A worm hardly wants to draw down into its burrow very hot or cold water lying on the surface of the beach at low tide.

The other two worms are commonest where the cockle is most nu-merous. *Axiothella quadrimaculata* (Figure 132), a bamboo worm, forms a narrow U-shaped tube of fine sand, so fragile that all efforts to remove it intact fail. The tail end of the tube projects well above the surface of the beach. The thin, cylindrical body has two distinct regions, the front, the smaller, of very short segments, the rear of longer ones. The head end is flat and sloping with a prominent rim, notched on each side; the hind end is funnel-shaped with a row of finger-like processes around the rim. The segments bear paired swellings which carry the bristles: these swellings are very large posteriorly and look like the nodes of a bamboo stem. It is greyish turquoise with the front region banded alternately with dark brown and cream; the swellings on the narrower hind part are brown and cream. Extremely elastic, this worm can be stretched to a fine thread (it often is when you are digging it out) before breaking. When everted, the 'throat' forms a soft, folded proboscis and this is used, as in *Abarenicola affinis*, to loosen and ingest the deposit.

Travisia olens (Figure 133) is the third of these deposit eating worms. Soon identified by its sickly odour, it has a short, plump body, pointed at each end and is dirty white; along each side is a row of long, retractable, thread-like gills, red with blood. The proboscis is like that of *Axiothella*.

Scavenging and carnivorous worms wander about the middle beach looking for food. They usually eat other bristle worms, small crustacea, pieces of organic matter which are held and swallowed with the proboscis. Most common and easy to recognize are *Glycera americana* and *Aglaophamus macroura*. *Glycera* (Figure 134) is pale grey with a pinkish tinge, long, round in section and finely pointed at each end: the tentacles at the tip of the front end are very small. It is identified by the way it coils its body tightly and by the long proboscis, armed with four strong, black jaws, which is suddenly shot out and then withdrawn. *Aglaophamus* (Figure 135) is shorter than *Glycera* and squarish in section: it is cream with a striking iridescence. Like *Glycera*, its movements are very characteristic and make on the spot identification very easy; it swims (inefficiently for the effort) or burrows into the deposit by throwing the body into very regular waves which pass forwards rapidly. *Aglaophamus* too has a large protrusible proboscis; the free end is encircled by several rows of papillae and just inside the opening are two horny jaws.

Two snails are common inhabitants of the lower part of the middle beach zone. One of them is the whelk *Cominella adspersa* (Figure 136), a close relative of *C. glandiformis* of the mudflat. The shell is somewhat plump and heavy, roughened by fine ridges and low humps and has a dull finish: the outside is fawn with regularly spaced dashes of dark brown along the ridges and the edge of the aperture is yellow and glossy. The body is dark grey spotted with opaque white. Active even when the tide is out, it can be found crawling about the shallow pools searching for carrion and living cockles: the soft parts of the bivalve are reached in the same way as in *Cominella glandiformis*. The other snail is *Baryspira australis* (Figure 137), an olive shell. The shell has smooth lines and a glossy finish, and is prettily coloured, being dark brown with narrow bands of blue, white and fawn. When the animal is active, flaps of skin from the broad foot envelope much of the shell and, with the blade-like head, form a streamlined shape, ideal for cutting a shallow trench as it moves along the surface. At the front end is a long mobile breathing tube which is part of the direction finding equipment used by the animal in its hunt for prey. Soft and smooth, the white skin is marbled violet brown; this pigment is very dense on the siphon.

The lower shore (the spring flat), only to be reached during spring

139. *Upogebia danai*, a mud shrimp, lives in a permanent burrow rather similar to that of *Callianassa*, a male and female (has an extra pair of abdominal limbs) together. The large, hairy first legs (extending forwards in the photograph) and the smaller second pair (obscured) form the sieve used to strain food (detritus) from the water current created by the swimming limbs on the underside of the abdomen: when feeding the mud shrimp moves close to the opening of its burrow. Length up to 5 cm.

tides, is an exciting place to dig, for here you will find the greatest variety of beach inhabitants. Limited space prevents us from describing more than just a handful of these. Although we have chosen animals which you can be sure of finding on any suitable beach, our selection is still a fair introduction to the diverse fauna of the lowest zone.

Two small crustaceans of the lower beach zone, common and easy to recognize, are *Callianassa filholi*, a ghost shrimp, and *Upogebia danai*, a mud shrimp. Though called shrimps they have closer affinity with the lobsters and hermit crabs because the body is flattened, the first abdominal segment small and the nippers are heavier than the first walking legs. *Callianassa* (Figure 138), so frail and weak when dug out of the deposit, is in water as active and agile as *Lysiosquilla*. The nippers have the shape normal for a crab or shrimp and in the male one of them (left or right) is very large. The body and limbs are transparent and colourless except for touches of vermilion. Its burrow is quite elaborate, consisting of a branching system of tunnels, with sections enlarged here and there for turning and side rooms for storing faeces and pieces of shell, joined to the surface by several vertical shafts. Water is circulated

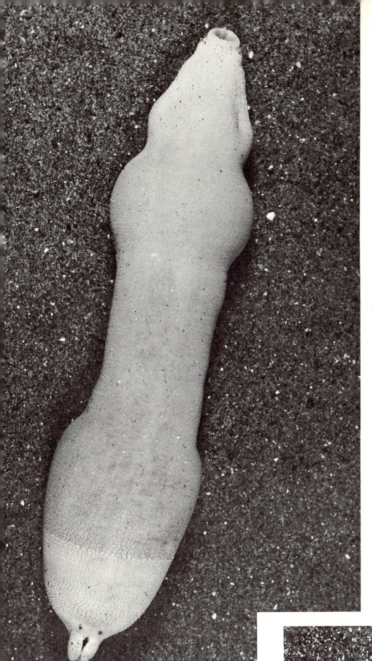

141. *Urechis novaezelandiae*, a tongue worm (a species which lives on the West Coast of North America is called the fat innkeeper, a very apt name since it shares its burrow with a scale worm, a pea crab and a fish). The animal in the photograph is lying on its back: it is in active state, the outline distorted by waves of contraction (these pass rearwards); when quiet, it is sausage-shaped. At one end is the short proboscis or 'tongue' with the single pair of strong, hooked bristles just behind; the anus, wide open, is at the other end and is surrounded by a ring of bristles. This worm breathes by continually taking water into the enlarged rectum and then expelling it. The tongue worm is occasional in occurrence on muddy sand beaches; the openings of the deep U-shaped burrow (up to 50 cm. deep) are wide and raised. Length up to 23 cm.

142. *Xenosiphon mundanus*, a peanut worm (the common name is more appropriate when applied to the related *Dendrostomum aeneum*). The characteristic criss-cross pattern of grooves, a good identification mark, and the introvert are well-shown in the photograph. Although needing confirmation, it does seem that this worm selects fine organic matter from the deposit for food. *Xenosiphon* is fairly rare on muddy sand beaches. Length up to 30 cm.

through the burrow by the owner standing at one of the junctions and beating its swimming limbs in the direction of one of the exits, Digging is done with the first, second and third pairs of walking limbs and the spoil is carried to the entrance held in the last pair of mouth appendages. For food, the ghost shrimp scrapes away with the hairy first walking legs, the lining of its burrow, rich in organic debris and small organisms brought from the sea outside in the water current created by itself. These scrapings are passed to the last of the mouth appendages, here broken into small crumbs and handed on to the limbs around the mouth which are used to sift out the finest. The residue of the meal is released into the water current and carried out through one of the outlets of the burrow.

Upogebia danai (Figure 139) is quickly distinguished from *Callianassa* by its pale orange brown colouration, small nippers (though still bigger than the walking legs) which are only partly formed (the immovable finger is very short) and the hairy 'cap' on its head. *Upogebia* builds a permanent burrow with turning chambers and two openings. It digs like the ghost shrimp but carries the spoil to the surface with the nippers. Food, detritus and small plants, is strained out with the hairy first and second legs from the water driven through the burrow by the beating of the swimming legs.

The bristle worms which we have described for the middle shore also live in the lower zone, though some of them, for example *Abarenicola affinis*, may not be quite so common. Accompanying them is another bristle worm of the tube-dwelling kind, *Pectinaria australis* (Figure 140). This worm differs from most of the others, however, by carrying its tube with it as it moves, ever so slowly, through the deposit. The tube is one of the most exquisite pieces of building to be seen in the whole of the animal (excluding man, of course) world; it is fragile, fairly long and tapered (sometimes slightly curved), open at both ends, and built of a mosaic of sand (one grain thick). When building the tube, the worm carefully selects each sand grain and then, with great precision, fits and cements it in place. *Pectinaria* lives shallowly and obliquely buried with the narrow (rear) end of the tube projecting slightly from the surface of the beach (it is sometimes hidden by a mound of faeces). At the buried wide end the head projects into the muddy sand; it bears two groups or 'combs' of large, slightly curved, golden bristles and numerous extensible tentacles. Immediately behind the head are two pairs of little comb-like gills, bright red with blood (the rest of the body is white or pale pink). This worm uses the strong bristles as a

112

101. *Ocnus brevidentis*, a small sea-cucumber. Sometimes quite common in clear waters, it inhabits the under surfaces of rocks and kelp holdfasts. The animal photographed has extended fully some of its feeding tentacles (the yellow and grey branched processes). Many of the tube feet are tipped with scarlet. Length up to 20 mm.

102. *Stichopus mollis*, the common sea-cucumber. Occasional specimens are encountered at or near low tide mark on coarse sand and broken shell between and under loose rocks, and at the bottom of large pools: it is much commoner subtidally. The feeding tentacles, partially protruded, are just visible at the head end (on the left). If greatly irritated, *Stichopus* will cast out its viscera through the anus; the reason for this rather drastic action is not known. Length up to 18 cm.

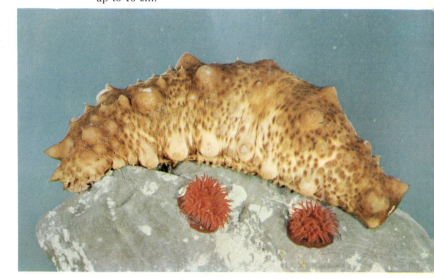

105. *Coscinasterias calamaria*, the eleven armed starfish. Smallish specimens of this starfish live on lower shore of most reefs sheltered from heavy waves. The common name is something of a misnomer since specimens do not always have eleven arms; the animal in the photograph has nine. *Coscinasterias* varies in colour from brown to bluish grey. Arm-spread up to 30 cm.

HIGH TIDE SPRINGS

UPPER SHORE   MIDDLE SHORE   LOWER SHORE

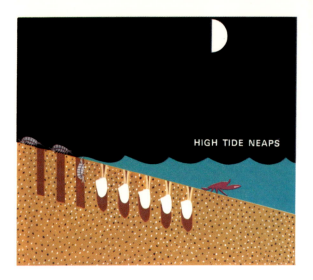

HIGH TIDE NEAPS

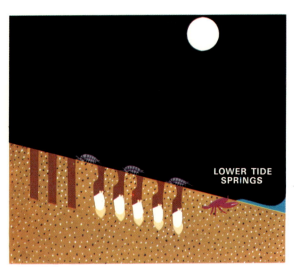

LOWER TIDE SPRINGS

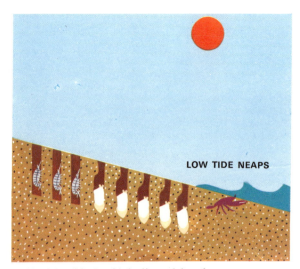

LOW TIDE NEAPS

106. Beach zonation: the three life zones (as described in this book) indicated by the distribution of certain animals across a sandy beach. EHWS — EXTREME HIGH WATER SPRINGS, ELWS — EXTREME LOW WATER SPRINGS. The indicator animals are: 1, upper shore — a sandhopper (*Talorchestia quoyana*), 2, middle shore — a clam (the toheroa, *Amphidesma ventricosum*), and 3, lower shore – a large crustacean (the common swimming crab, *Ovalipes punctatus*). The four panels show, in a simplified way, that the activity of the indicator animals varies with the time of day and state of tide.

fork to loosen and turn over the deposit, collecting with the tentacles, as it digs, particles for food and tube building. By removing particles, a cavern is excavated and the roof of this often partially collapses. Water is circulated through the cavern and tube, seemingly either way; the current is probably created by the rhythmical beating of flap-like processes (parapodia) on the sides of the body. The passage of this current probably enriches the deposit in the feeding area, small organisms and detritus being strained off. *Pectinaria* can withdraw into its tube and close the two openings, the front with the bristles and the rear with a small lobe over the anus.

Two interesting and unusual worms of the lowest beach zone are *Urechis novaezelandiae* and *Xenosiphon mundanus*. *Urechis novaezelandiae* (Figure 141), a tongue or spoon worm, is like a large, fat sausage, dirty white or pale pink in colour and textured rather like the skin of the domestic pig, with a small scoop-like proboscis at the front end and a ring of bright, golden bristles at the rear. The burrow goes deep and is U-shaped with an opening at the tip of each limb or shaft. Water is pumped through the burrow, for respiration and feeding, by alternate waves of swelling and constriction passing along the body rearwards. Organic matter and small organisms are strained from the water current so created by a funnel-shaped net of mucus: the wide opening of this mucous funnel is fastened to the slimy lining of the burrow and the narrow opening to the front end of the worm (at the base of the proboscis). The worm breaks its connection and swallows the mucous funnel when it is loaded with food. *Xenosiphon mundanus* (Figure 142), a peanut worm, lives deep in an L- or U-shaped burrow. It is long, sausage-like, white and iridescent with the surface finely grooved in a lattice-like pattern. Like its relative *Dendrostomum aeneum*, there is a protrusible introvert at the front end; the stem of this organ is covered with tubercles which are probably used to dig the burrow, and the tip is frilled and edged with short finger-like processes. *Xenosiphon* feeds on organic matter present in the deposit: huge quantities of muddy sand, pushed into the mouth with the terminal frill of the proboscis, are passed through the gut.

Another soft-bodied inhabitant of the lower beach is *Balanoglossus australiensis* (Figure 143), an acorn worm. Though very worm-like in appearance, *Balanoglossus* is not a worm; it is related to the sea-squirts but their connection can only be recognized from certain features of the internal structure. Because the acorn worm is fragile, great care must be taken when removing it from its burrow. The bright yellow front end is easy to see, but the rear end is so transparent and delicate that it is almost invisible against the muddy sand. The long body is divided into three regions: first the bulbous proboscis or 'acorn' which is very mobile and plastic, then the thick collar or 'cup' (the mouth opens inside this), followed by the long trunk; the trunk also has three parts, the wide front part with wing-like processes (the gill pouches open on the inside), the narrower, short middle with a row of hemispherical swellings ('liver' pouches) on each side, and the rear, long, cylindrical and pimply. *Balanoglossus* lives in a U-shaped burrow, open at the tip of each limb. The burrow is dug and shaped with the proboscis: this organ is first extended, then a swelling is formed which travels rearward and eventually serves to anchor the body for the next forward extension. The mucous lining of the burrow is secreted by the proboscis. Fine particles are collected with the proboscis when it is thrust out of the opening of the head shaft of the burrow (when the tide is in); beating cilia pass these particles, trapped in mucus, to the stalk of the proboscis where they are formed into cords and these are slowly drawn in through the mouth. Large quantities of particles are collected and swallowed; many are of no food value (selection is by size) except for a coating of organic substance and are voided as waste, deposited in a thick cord just outside the opening of the tail shaft.

The ostrich foot, *Struthiolaria papulosa* (Figure 144), is a really choice example of the rich fauna of the lower shore. It is probably the rarest of the animals described but it is so attractive and interesting that we just cannot leave it out. It is a largish snail: the shell is fairly heavy, distinctly shouldered with a row of prominent knobs along the edge, and is white with uneven stripes of grey and delicate reddish lilac or reddish brown; the aperture is bounded by thick lips, glossy and greyish yellow, the inner lip purplish red above and below and the outer edged with dark purple. The body and tentacles are reddish orange. *Struthiolaria* lies buried just below the surface of the beach, the body and shell horizontal. A short vertical shaft to the surface, made and maintained by the very mobile and extensible snout, provides the inlet for the water current (created by the cilia of the gills). As in the bivalves, respiration and feeding are combined; particles filtered out on the gill are fashioned, with mucus, into a cord which is gradually carried along a groove to the right side of the head; periodically the animal bends its snout to bite off pieces of this nutritious cord. Water flowing out of the gill cavity passes to the surface through another vertical shaft, sited posteriorly to the inlet.

114

Echinoderms are well represented on the lower beach. *Astropecten polyacanthus* (Figure 145), a comb star, moves about slowly just below the surface: it buries itself by digging out a shallow hole with the tube feet, turning up the sides of the arms so that the excavated deposit can be tossed aside. Unlike other sea-stars, *Astropecten* has tube feet which are suckerless (suckers are not very useful on an unstable surface); however, this sea-star moves along just like its rock dwelling relatives (the stepping of adjacent feet does not seem to be synchronized). *Astropecten* is very regular in shape and fairly stiff, though the top is soft; along the sides are large, sharp spines. Greyish yellow marked with dark brown, it is hard to see against the muddy sand. Unlike the other sea-stars we have described, *Astropecten* swallows its prey, mostly small snails and bivalves, whole, taking in large quantities of deposit at the same time.

If you scan the surface carefully as you walk across the lower shore, you may see groups of short worm-like creatures, wriggling as they poke out of the deposit. Taking a closer look you will discover that they are not worms but the tips of the arms of a brittle-star, *Monamphiura aster* (Figure 146). The disc-shaped body, burnt umber or fawn in colour, is deeply buried, right way up, and two or three of the very long arms, pink and brown banded, reach up and through the surface of the beach. One of these arms is waved up and down and this creates a current of water which is used to aerate the burrow. Two arms always remain buried, one is arched to support the roof of the chamber in which the body lies, the other is thrust out horizontally into the sediment to collect food, the fine particles being transported along it to the mouth by the tube feet.

The two sea-urchins which live here do not look like each other or their cousin the sea-egg (*Evechinus chloroticus*). *Echinocardium australe* (Figure 147), a heart urchin, is, as the common name implies, heart-shaped. The straw coloured spines are small, slender, very numerous and of several different sizes; the tube feet are arranged in two groups, upper and lower, not in neat, complete tracts as in the sea-egg. The body is distorted so that the anus is near one end and the mouth close to the other, both on the lower (oral) surface. A deep burrower, the heart urchin keeps its subterranean home aerated through a vertical shaft which is fashioned and maintained by the long tube feet of the upper surface. At the rear end of the animal there is a recess in the wall of the burrow, made by the tube feet just below the anus, and here the faeces are dumped. Using the paddle-shaped lower spines, the heart

115

109. *Scyphax ornatus*, an isopod or sea-slater which lives on sand beaches at the same level as the sandhopper: it is not as common (up to 20/m²). *Scyphax* can burrow as deeply as the sandhopper — the depth it penetrates to depends on the dampness of the sand (neither sea-slater nor sandhopper has control over water loss). Not all individuals are nocturnal: tiny animals forage across the beach during the day. Length up to 25 mm.

114. *Alpheus* sp., a snapping shrimp. Restricted to the harbours of the northern 'finger' of the North Island, this snapping shrimp (up to 10/m.²) burrows, often quite deeply, into the wet mud of flats, eel-grass beds and, further up the shore, mangrove swamps. It feeds on fine organic debris which it collects and sorts with the larger mouth appendages; like some of its overseas relatives, it probably takes live prey such as amphipods or shrimps, stunning them with the large nipper. Length up to 6 cm.

115. *Lysiosquilla spinosa*, a mantis shrimp: the animal shown is a male; the female is distinguished by a wide, dull red band down the middle of the back. This mantis shrimp forms a burrow, a vertical shaft, in flats of firm mud from mid tide level down; it leaves its burrow for a short time only and then usually at night. Length up to 75 mm.

118. *Nucula hartvigiana*, a nut shell, is often found with, and is sometimes as abundant as, the cockle (*Chione stutchburyi*): it has not, however, such a wide range over the flat and is also rather patchy in distribution, showing a preference for wet mud. Length (of the shell) up to 7·5 mm.

121. *Cominella glandiformis*, a whelk, is very common on mudflats, less so on muddy sand beaches (usually restricted on these to the middle shore, being replaced lower down by the closely related *Cominella adspersa*). It is randomly spread over the flat except when it forms groups, sometimes quite large, around food such as living cockles, pipis and dead fish. Food can be detected (using the breathing tube or siphon and special smell organ inside the respiratory chamber), even when there is just a film of water, from up to 30 metres away. When food is detected, the whelk bends its siphon (can be seen projecting from the front end of the shell in the animal photographed) to determine the location. A whelk reaches the soft parts of a living cockle with its proboscis either through an opening where the edge of the prey's shell is chipped or by wedging open the prey's shell with the lip of its own shell. Height (of the shell) up to 25 mm.

112. *Ovalipes catharus*, the common swimming crab. A low tidal inhabitant of surf beaches, it spends much of the day buried (except for the eyes and feelers) just below the surface, awaiting prey. It emerges to swim mainly at night. As well as feeding on dead animals, it also attacks living tuatuas and ghost shrimps. Width of the body up to 85 mm.

134. *Glycera americana*, a bristle worm (sometimes called, erroneously, the blood worm), is shown in its characteristic coiled pose which it assumes when removed from the deposit. A predacious worm feeding principally on amphipods and small bristle worms: the hard parts of the meal are regurgitated once digestion is complete. This worm inhabits muddy sand beaches, mudflats and eel-grass beds. Length up to 18 cm.

135. *Aglaophamus macroura*, a bristle worm. A very active, predacious worm, it moves (throwing its body into regular waves — see the photograph) through the deposit searching for a meal. A common inhabitant, from mean tide level down, of muddy sand beaches, *Aglaophamus* occasionally occurs in sandy beaches and eel-grass beds. Length up to 15 cm.

116

Figure 109   See facing page

Figure 114   See facing page

Figure 118   See facing page

Figure 115   See facing page

Figure 112   See facing page

Figure 121   See facing page

123. *Zediloma subrostrata*, the mudflat top shell. This snail crawls easily over soft mud, though it does show a preference for firmer surfaces such as stones, pieces of shell, bottles, old car tyres, bedsteads and eel-grass beds. It is quickly distinguished from its close relatives of rocky shores *Zediloma atrovirens*, *Z. arida* and *Z. digna* by the ridged shell, yellowish marked with oblique purple lines. Height (of the shell) up to 15 mm.

131. *Abarenicola affinis*, a lugworm. The most obvious features of the worm photographed are the two distinct regions of the body (the trunk with paired gills and the narrower tail), the bristle bearing appendages which are used to grip the deposit, and the three prominent ring-like swellings near the front end which are formed to anchor the body during digging movements. This bristle worm occurs in muddy sand beaches and banks in Otago, Lyttelton, Wellington and Manukau Harbours. Length up to 15 cm.

132. *Axiothella quadrimaculata*, a bamboo worm (sometimes called a joint worm), is recognized by the prominent well-spaced swellings, which bear bristles, and the head-plate at the front end of the trunk (the curled brown and cream part). *Axiothella* is common over the lower half of muddy sand beaches. Length up to 15 cm.

Figure 134   See page 116

133. *Travisia olens*, a bristle worm. Obvious marks of identification are the thick short body, pointed at the head end, the row of filamentous red gills along each side and the unpleasant smell. Although rather localized in distribution, it is usually very abundant. *Travisia olens* has been recorded south to Moeraki (the South Island). Length up to 9 cm.

Figure 135   See page 116

Figure 136　See next text page

Figure 137　See next text page

Figure 138　See next text page

Figure 140　See next text page

Figure 143　See next text page

Figure 144　See next text page

147. *Echinocardium australe*, a heart urchin, lives buried at about the same depth as *Monamphiura* with which it is often found. Like this brittle-star, the heart urchin can re-bury itself very quickly, digging in with the side spines. The upper surface of the heart urchin is shown: the spines are directed rearwards to streamline the body for burrowing; the large tube feet (not extended here) which make the respiratory shaft of the burrow arise from the deep, wide groove guarded by the long spines. Length up to 4 cm.

145. *Astropecten polyacanthus*, a comb star, rests shallowly buried in the substrate when it is not feeding. Although it favours shellfish as food, this starfish or sea-star will also eat the heart urchin *Echinocardium australe*; buried prey is located with considerable precision. *Astropecten* is unable to dig down to animals which live deeply buried. The animal shown has turned over one of its arms and the suckerless tube feet are visible. This starfish lives at low tide mark on muddy sand beaches. Arm-spread up to 20 cm.

146. *Monamphiura aster*, a brittle-star, lies quite deeply buried (about 10 cm. down) in the beach. It can bury itself in less than two minutes; the tube feet on the underside of the arms flick aside the particles of sand and mud and the arms are flexed sideways and thrust into the deposit. The burrow of this brittle-star is only a temporary one; it digs itself a new one as it moves slowly (in the direction of the horizontal feeding arm — see the text) through the deposit. A low tidal inhabitant of muddy sand beaches. Arm-spread up to 29 cm.

148. *Arachnoides zelandiae*, a sea-biscuit (known locally as the snapper biscuit), unlike the heart urchin buries itself only shallowly. It can be found in moderate numbers at low tide mark on muddy sand and sand beaches. Diameter up to 10 cm.

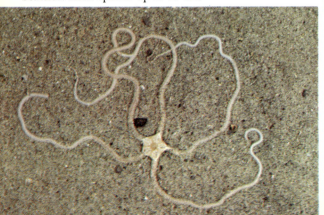

Captions for colour plates 136, 137, 138, 140, 143, 144

136. *Cominella adspersa*, the speckled whelk, is the dominant predacious snail of the lower shore on muddy sand beaches. Higher up the shore it is replaced by *Cominella glandiformis* (which also lives on mudflats); where these two species of whelk overlap they often feed together; the cockle prey, it seems, is usually opened by the large *Cominella adspersa* (in the way described for *C. glandiformis* — see the legend to Figure 121). The speckled whelk has been observed feeding on the bivalve *Myadora striata* and the southern olive, *Baryspira australis*. Length (of the shell) up to 50 mm.

137. *Baryspira australis*, the southern olive. The photograph shows an animal in crawling attitude; the shell is partly covered by flaps of the foot and the tubular siphon is fully extended forwards (this siphon is used for breathing and prey detection as in the whelks). This olive shell is not uncommon on muddy sand beaches, particularly near low tide; occasionally it occurs in sand. It is found south to Sumner (near Christchurch). Height (of the shell) up to 34 mm.

138. *Callianassa filholi*, a ghost shrimp, forms a permanent burrow, often quite complex with several shafts to the surface ('entrance' hole at the bottom of a depression, 'exit' at the top of a low mound); a burrow is usually occupied by a male and a female. The animal in the photograph is a male; the female has small, equal nippers and an enlarged second abdominal segment. The ghost shrimp spends a lot of time cleaning itself with the brush-like tips of the fifth pair of legs. It is quite frequent from mean tide level down on beaches of muddy sand, less so on sand. Length up to 6 cm.

140. *Pectinaria australis*, a comb worm, lives inside its sand tube, obliquely buried, head downwards in the deposit. In the photograph the worm has protruded its head (which it does when digging and feeding) and the 'combs', each a row of enlarged bristles, and two pairs of red gills are displayed. *Pectinaria* is sometimes quite common in muddy sand. Length up to 5 cm.

143. *Balanoglossus australiensis*, an acorn worm. As far as is known, this animal has a rather restricted distribution in New Zealand; it is recorded only for the Hauraki Gulf where it is common on muddy sand beaches. The mode of life of the acorn worm would seem to parallel that of the lugworm *Abarenicola affinis* (not recorded for the Hauraki Gulf) except its activities are not so rhythmic and it is dominant at a much lower level (the lower shore). Length up to 15 cm.

144. *Struthiolaria papulosa*, the ostrich foot or kaikaikaroro, is a sea snail much favoured as a food by Maoris. The body of the animal photographed is only partly protruded, but the characteristic fine, tapered tentacles, the short, stout foot and operculum with sharp point are clearly visible. The ostrich foot is fairly rare near low tide mark on muddy sand beaches. Height (of the shell) up to 83 mm.

urchin slowly pushes itself forwards through the deposit, extending and reshaping its burrow as it goes. Particles, both organic and inorganic, are passed to the mouth by the tube feet associated with it or by the beating of cilia over most of the surface of the body. *Arachnoides zelandiae* (Figure 148), a biscuit urchin or sea-biscuit, locally called the snapper biscuit, is circular and flattened (the lower surface is flat, the upper a very low cone) and densely covered with small spines. The tube feet are tiny and numerous, and in narrow rows. The snapper biscuit walks across the surface or buries itself just below. It digs in quite rapidly, entering the beach obliquely and banking up the deposit at the front; the hind end is often left uncovered. Like the heart urchin, *Arachnoides* feeds on fine organic particles; as the animal burrows these fall between the spines onto the surface of the body and are carried by ciliary currents to the mouth.

Trochodota dendyi (Figure 149), a burrowing sea cucumber, is easily mistaken for a worm. Its body is long and circular in section and the body wall is thin, transparent, colourless or faintly pink, and marked by five lines (thicker regions of the body wall); there are no tube feet. A ring of tentacles (each fringed with delicate, finger-like processes) surrounds the mouth. Head first, *Trochodota* burrows obliquely into the beach pushing the deposit aside by muscular contractions of the body; the rear end lies close to the opening of the burrow. It feeds simply by pushing muddy sand into the mouth with its tentacles.

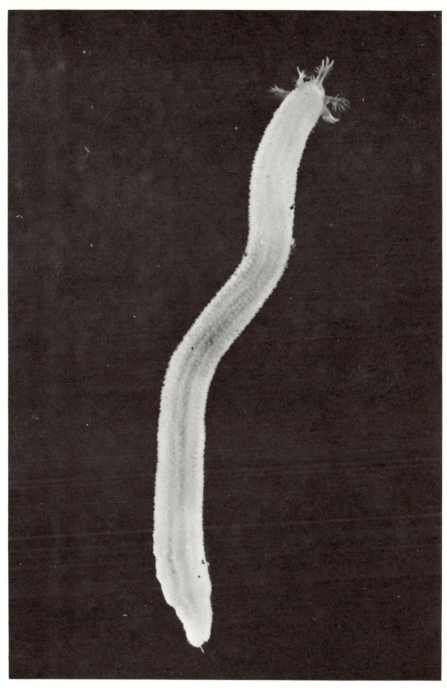

149. *Trochodota dendyi*, a sea-cucumber, is a low tidal species of muddy sand beaches; it burrows to a depth of about 20 cm., head downwards. Visible in the animal shown are the feeding tentacles surrounding the mouth, some of them extended and showing the finger-like side processes, and the papillae of the skin (supported by minute hook-like elements) which are used to grip the wall of the burrow during digging. Length up to 15 cm.

Further Reading

To those who wish to make a more extensive tour of the subject of local seashore life, we recommend that they take as their guide *The New Zealand Sea Shore* by J.E. Morton and M.C. Miller. Not only does this book describe and explore, graphically and in a deeper and more expansive manner, the organisms and phenomena considered by us, it describes and discusses many others as well. Also, this book serves as a signpost to the sources of much of our knowledge and thinking, for it lists many of the articles and books which present original observations, describe experiments, or generate ideas, on or about shore organisms, particularly those living in New Zealand waters.

You may want to compare our seashores with those of other lands. There are so many books on overseas shores that we can mention here only a select few. Australian shore life, probably of greatest interest because of its similarity to our own, is well described in the late W.J. Dakin's *Australian seashores* (1952, Angus and Robertson). The Pacific coast of North America, much further away though in the same ocean, is admirably portrayed in the late E.F. Ricketts (on whom John Steinbeck modelled 'Doc' of *Cannery Row*) and J. Calvin's *Between Pacific Tides* (third edition published in 1952, Stanford University Press); Dr Joel Hedgpeth, a famous American marine biologist who revised the later editions of this book, has added pocket reviews, many of them very witty, on the best known works on marine science including most of those mentioned here. Not so relevant to our shores in the particulars but very much so in the generalities is Sir Maurice Yonge's *The Sea Shore* (1949, Collins); this is certainly the finest book of its kind and should be read by all who are interested in the shore.

What about sea life beyond the shore? Though there are a great many books about this, only one of these concerns our coastal waters. This book is Wade Doak's *Beneath New Zealand Seas* (1971, Reed), a delightful account of the startlingly colourful, often bizarrely shaped, organisms which inhabit subtidal rock. Unfortunately, there are no equivalent works for the naturalist about organisms either living on other types of sea bottom (sand, mud or gravel and shell) or floating or swimming in the water above (the plankton). Undoubtedly the best introduction to these habitats are Sir Alister Hardy's two books, lucidly written and beautifully illustrated, called *The Open Sea* (based mainly on our knowledge of North Atlantic waters), Volume I being entitled *The World of Plankton* (1956, Collins) and Volume II *Fish and Fisheries* (1959, Collins).

Some readers may prefer one book which covers all of the aspects of sea life considered separately in the works already mentioned. To these people we recommend that they select either *The Sea* (second edition 1963, Frederick Warne) by Sir Frederick Russell and Sir Maurice Yonge or L. Engel's book of the same title published in the Life Nature Library (1961).

Classification

Although all of the main groups of living organisms are listed, only those which contain the species met with in this book are defined and then only very briefly and simply; these groups are subdivided only when it is necessary to distinguish well-known forms e.g. crabs, shrimps, sea-slaters, sandhoppers etc. within the class Crustacea. Kingdom, phylum, class and order, and smaller divisions of each indicated by the prefix sub-, are terms for some of the principal levels of classification; the lower the level, closer is the similarity, and relationship (assuming that evolution has taken place), between all of the member species. Of the other three major divisions, two, the family and the genus, are not used here; the third, the species, is of course, employed wherever a scientific name (composed of two words e.g. *Dendrodoris*, the generic name, *citrina*, the trivial name) is given.

KINGDOM PLANTAE

Sub-kingdom Thallophyta

Simple in structure, no roots, stems or leaves.
The following eight phyla are known as the Algae (although alga is the Latin for a seaweed, not all of the members of the group live in the sea). All of these phyla include members with the green pigment chlorophyll (this pigment captures the energy of visible light for photosynthesis).

PHYLUM CYANOPHYTA, the blue-green algae.
Possibly the simplest of the plants, a single cell, a group of cells or filaments (each a row of cells); unlike other algae the nuclear material (concerned with functioning and inheritance) and pigment (light fixing) present within the cells is not in discrete bodies; live on the bottom, but may creep along (by the production of mucilage). e.g. *Calothrix scopulorum*.

PHYLUM PYRROPHYTA, the dinoflagellates.
Usually a single cell with a heavy wall sometimes sculptured to form plates; two flagella, one across the body, the other projecting rearwards; free-swimming. e.g. *Gymnodinium brevis.*

PHYLUM CHRYSOPHYTA, the yellowish-green and the golden brown algae, and the diatoms. A single cell, groups of cells or filaments; recognised by the substances stored.
Class BACILLARIOPHYCEAE, the diatoms.
Without flagella, cell wall of two distinct pieces which fit together, one overlapping the other. e.g. *Coscinodiscus concinnus.*
Other classes are the Xanthophyceae, Chrysophyceae and Haptophyceae – the last two include many of the microflagellates.

PHYLUM CHLOROPHYTA, the green algae (includes the green seaweeds and some of the microflagellates). A single cell (some have flagella and swim), filaments (simple or branched) or a membrane (sometimes divided); store starch and are green pigmented. e.g. *Enteromorpha intestinalis, Ulva lactuca.*

PHYLUM PHAEOPHYTA, the brown algae (brown seaweeds).
Filaments or a membrane of several layers of cells, most are large and distinctively shaped; green pigment is present but masked by brown pigment. e.g. *Carpophyllum maschalocarpum, Hormosira banksii.*

PHYLUM RHODOPHYTA, the red algae (red seaweeds).
A single cell, filaments or a membrane of several layers of cells, solid and distinctively shaped; green pigment present but masked by red pigment (sometimes purple or pink). e.g. *Gigartina circumcincta, Plocamium costatum.*

The other two phyla of algae, the Euglenophyta and the Cryptophyta, include microflagellates of the plankton.
The following three phyla of the Thallophyta are known as the Fungi. No chlorophyll.

PHYLUM EUMYCOPHYTA, the true fungi.
Body composed of threads (hyphae).
Several classes including
Class Lichenes, the lichens.
Composed of a fungus and an alga, living in partnership. e.g. *Xanthoria parietina.*

123

Other phyla of the Fungi are the Schizomycophyta (the bacteria) and the Myxomycophyta (the slime moulds).

Sub-kingdom Embryophyta

Chlorophyll present; an embryo is formed in the female sex organ.

PHYLUM BRYOPHYTA, the liverworts and mosses.
No vascular tissue.

PHYLUM TRACHEOPHYTA

Vascular tissue (for circulation of the sap) present.
Several sub-phyla including the
Sub-phylum Pteropsida

Relatively large leaves with many, often branched, veins.

Three classes
Class ANGIOSPERMAE, the flowering plants.
Seeds enclosed in an ovary which ripens into a fruit.
e.g. *Avicennia resinifera, Zostera nana.*
The other two classes are the Filicineae (the ferns) and the Gymnospermae (the cycads, ginkgos and conifers).

KINGDOM ANIMALIA

Sub-kingdom and phylum Protozoa

Body not divided into cells, but is usually more complex than any single cell of the higher animals.

Class MASTIGOPHORA, the flagellates.
Many of the flagellates (micro- and dino-) included here amongst the algae are often placed by zoologists in this protozoan class.

Class RHIZOPODA, includes the famous amoeba.

Other classes are the Sporozoa (all are parasites) and the Ciliophora (includes the well-known *Paramecium*).

Sub-kingdom and phylum Parazoa, the sponges.

Live attached to the substratum; the body, very plastic in shape, is rather like a complex colony of protozoans; though many-celled there are no tissues or organs like the Metazoa; there is a system of cavities with entrances and exits, but there is no gut in the true sense.

Class CALCAREA
A fairly simple system of cavities; spicules (forming the skeleton) of calcium carbonate. e.g. *Leucosolenia* sp.

Class DEMOSPONGIAE
A complex system of cavities; spicules, if present, of silica; skeleton may be of fibres or absent.
e.g. *Tethya aurantium.*

The other class is the Hexactinellida.

Sub-kingdom and phylum Mesozoa.

Minute parasites of the excretory organs of the squids and octopuses. Body very simple (a coat of ciliated cells surrounding a reproductive cell).

Sub-kingdom Metazoa

Many-celled, cells arranged into tissues and, excepting the first phylum, the tissues are arranged into organs.

PHYLUM COELENTERATA

Radially symmetrical (built on a circular plan like a car or bicycle wheel), two layers of cells (Diploblastica) with a jelly-like layer (mesoglea) containing scattered cells in between: gut with one opening.

Sub-phylum Cnidaria
Nematocysts present.

Class HYDROZOA
Polyp (flower-like, mouth surrounded by one or more circles of tentacles) and medusa (jellyfish) stages usually present in life-cycle.
Order Hydroida, the sea-firs or hydroids and the hydras. Polyp and medusa of roughly equal importance.
e.g. *Obelia longissima.*
Several other orders, the best known being the Siphonophora
e.g. *Physalia physalis* (Portuguese man-o'-war).

Class SCYPHOZOA, the true jellyfish.
Medusa stage prominent.

Class ANTHOZOA
Polyp stage only (polyp larger, more complex in structure than the comparable stage in the Hydrozoa).

Sub-class Alcyonaria, the soft corals, sea-pens, sea-fans and false corals.
Eight pinnate tentacles e.g. *Alcyonium aurantiacum* (Dead man's fingers).

125

Sub-class Zoantharia, the sea-anemones and stony corals.
Tentacles simple, six or multiples of six. e.g. *Actinia tenebrosa, Isactinia olivacea.*

Sub-phylum Ctenophora, the comb-jellies.
Lassoo cells instead of nematocysts. e.g. *Pleurobrachia pileus* (sea-gooseberry).

Rest of the phyla have three layers of cells (Triploblastica) and are basically bilaterally symmetrical (the body has two sides by virtue of having a head and tail, and an upper and lower surface); organs are present.

The following two phyla have no body cavity (Acoelomata) i.e. the organs are embedded in the middle layer.

PHYLUM PLATYHELMINTHES, the flatworms.
Gut with one opening on the underside.

Class TURBELLARIA, the free-living flatworms.
Skin with cilia; proboscis is part of the gut. e.g. *Thysanozoon brochii.*

Other classes are the Trematoda (the flukes) and the Cestoda (the tapeworms).

PHYLUM NEMERTEA, the ribbon worms.
Skin with cilia; gut with two openings (mouth and anus); proboscis separate from the gut. e.g. *Amphiporus* sp.

Other phyla at a similar level of structure, but with the organs lying in an unlined cavity (pseudocoel) are the Aschelminthes (five classes including the Nematoda, the roundworms, and the Nematomorpha, the horsehair worms), Acanthocephala, the spiny headed worms, Priapulida and Entoprocta.

All of the remaining phyla also have the organs lying in a cavity, but this cavity (coelom) differs from the pseudocoel in being lined with a layer of cells (the peritoneum) and in having a different embryonic origin.

PHYLUM ANNELIDA, the segmented worms.
Body segmented; skin has a thin coat (cuticle).

Class POLYCHAETA, the bristle worms.
Recognizable head; trunk segments typically have limb-like outgrowths (parapodia) provided with bristles. e.g. *Eulalia microphylla, Axiothella quadrimaculata.*

Other classes are the Oligochaeta (the earthworms), Hirudinea (the leeches), Archiannelida and Myzostomaria.

PHYLUM SIPUNCULIDA, the peanut worms.
No segmentation in the adult; front end invaginable. e.g. *Dendrostomum aeneum, Xenosiphon mundanus.*

PHYLUM ECHIURIDA, the tongue worms.
No segmentation in the adult; proboscis ('tongue') present in front of the mouth; a small number of bristles present. e.g. *Urechis novaezelandiae.*

PHYLUM ARTHROPODA
Segmented, jointed external skeleton of chitin; paired limbs on some or all of the segments: body cavity (coelom) reduced, replaced by an enlarged blood system).

Class CRUSTACEA
Head of six segments, trunk divisible into a thorax and abdomen; two pairs of feelers: skeleton is often calcified.

Sub-class Cirripedia, the barnacles.
Attached to the substratum at the head end; a carapace (backward projecting fold from the head) of several calcareous plates encloses the body; six pairs of legs, abdomen reduced. e.g. *Chamaesipho columna, Elminius modestus.*

Sub-class Malacostraca
Compound eyes, often stalked; typically the carapace covers the thorax of eight segments, abdomen of six segments.

Order Stomatopoda, the mantis shrimps.
Shallow carapace fused with three thoracic segments, four segments uncovered; first five limbs with a partial nipper. e.g. *Lysiosquilla spinosa.*

Order Peracarida
Carapace, if present, not fused with more than four thoracic segments.

Sub-order Isopoda, the wood-lice, pill-bugs and sea-slaters.
No carapace, body flattened from above downwards; legs all alike except the first pair; eyes not stalked. e.g. *Amphoroidea falcifer.*

Sub-order Amphipoda, the sandhoppers, shore-skippers and beach shrimps.

Body flattened from side to side; legs of more than one type; eyes not stalked. e.g. *Talorchestia quoyana.*

Other sub-orders are the Mysidacea, Cumacea and Tanaidacea.
Order Eucarida

Carapace fused with all of the thoracic segments; eyes with stalks.

Sub-order Decapoda, the shrimps, prawns, crayfish, hermit crabs and crabs.

Three pairs of legs modified as mouth appendages; five pairs of walking legs; usually more than one set of gills. e.g. *Alope spinifrons, Ozius truncatus.*

Other sub-order is the Euphausiacea, the krill (planktonic food of the whalebone whales).

Other sub-classes are the Branchiopoda (fairy shrimps, water fleas, clam shrimps etc.), Cephalocarida, Ostracoda (mussel shrimps), Copepoda (most important herbivores of the plankton), Mystacocarida and Branchiura (carp-lice).

Other classes of arthropods are the Onychophora (velvet worms), Pauropoda, Diplopoda (millepedes), Chilopoda (centipedes), Symphyla, Insecta (insects), Merostomata (king crabs or horseshoe crabs), Arachnida (scorpions, sun-spiders, whip scorpions, spiders, harvestmen, mites and ticks), Pycnogonida (sea-spiders), Pentastomida and Tardigrada (water bears).

PHYLUM MOLLUSCA

Body, clearly divisible into a head, foot and hump, is soft and unsegmented and usually protected by a shell (secreted by the mantle, a fold of skin on the hump); the gills lie in the cavity formed by the mantle: body cavity (coelom) reduced, viscera lie in a large blood space.

Class AMPHINEURA

Body long, mouth and anus at opposite ends; no tentacles or eyes.
Order Polyplacophora, the chitons or coat-of-mail shells.

Shell of eight, articulated pieces and a well-developed flat foot. e.g. *Ischnochiton maorianus, Amaurochiton glaucus.*

Other order is the Aplacophora.

Class GASTROPODA

Well-developed head with tentacles and eyes, hump twisted at some stage of development.

Sub-class Prosobranchia, the slit limpets, keyhole limpets, true limpets and sea snails.
Hump (often spirally coiled as is the shell) twisted so that the anus lies above the head; shell usually with an operculum; gills present. e.g. *Cellana radians, Nerita melanotragus, Lunella smaragda, Haliotis iris, Lamellaria ophione.*

Sub-class Opisthobranchia, the bubble shells, sea-hares and sea-slugs.
Hump partly or completely untwisted in the adult (anus now lies on the side or at the rear of the body); the shell is reduced or lost and the head usually bears two pairs of tentacles. e.g. *Haminoea zelandiae, Stiliger felinus, Dendrodoris citrina.*

Sub-class Pulmonata, the land snails, slugs and relatives.
Hump partly or, occasionally, completely untwisted, but often still spirally coiled as is the shell; usually no operculum, no gills and the mantle cavity is lung-like; head often bears two pairs of tentacles. e.g. *Amphibola crenata, Siphonaria zelandica.*

Class BIVALVIA, the bivalves.
Flattened from side to side with a shell of two pieces or valves (joined together by a ligament and usually hinged); palps (large ridged flaps flanking the mouth) present, gills large; head reduced, without tentacles or eyes.

Sub-class Protobranchia, the nutshells and awning shells.
Usually the palps are large, have a tentacle-like process (palp proboscis) and are used in feeding; the gills are small, composed of plate-like leaflets and are restricted to the hind part of the mantle cavity; the foot has a sole. e.g. *Nucula hartvigiana.*

Sub-class Lamellibranchia, the mussels, cockles, clams and scallops.
Palps small in comparison with the enlarged gills; the gill leaflets are filamentar and reflected (the gill is W-shaped in cross section); foot blade-like, no sole. e.g. *Chione stutchburyi Macomona liliana, Amphidesma australe.*

Other sub-class is the Septibranchia.

Other classes are the Monoplacophora, Scaphopoda (tusk shells) and Cephalopoda (squids and octopuses).

PHYLUM POLYZOA, the sea-mats.
Attached to the substratum, usually colonial; the body of an individual

is unsegmented and the mouth is surrounded by a circlet of tentacles which can be withdrawn into the zooecium (protective 'house', the hardened part of the body wall); the gut is U-shaped, the anus lying close to the mouth. e.g. *Hippothoa bougainvillei*.

Other phyla characterised by a crown of tentacles are the Brachiopoda (lamp shells) and the Phoronida.

PHYLUM ECHINODERMATA
Body is radially symmetrical in the adult (the larval stage shows bilateral symmetry), has calcareous plates in the body wall, possesses tube feet, and is sometimes armed with spines.

Class ASTEROIDEA, the starfish or sea-stars.
Star-shaped or pentagonal (five sides), the skeletal plates form a network or loose shell; there is a groove along the undersurface of each arm and the tube feet are usually tipped with a sucker; mouth without teeth. e.g. *Patiriella regularis, Coscinasterias calamaria*.

Class OPHIUROIDEA, the brittle-stars and basket-stars.
Star-shaped, slender arms (without grooves) sharply marked off from the central disc; skeleton of articulated plates; tube feet without a sucker and mouth armed with teeth. e.g. *Ophiopteris antipodum*.

Class ECHINOIDEA, the sea-urchins.
Body globular or flat; skeleton a shell (test) of fixed plates (spines movable); mouth sometimes armed with teeth; tube feet with a sucker. e.g. *Evechinus chloroticus*.

Class, HOLOTHUROIDEA, the sea-cucumbers.
Body sausage-shaped (bilateral symmetry superimposed on radial symmetry), soft, without spines; skeleton reduced to small plates scattered in the body wall; mouth encircled by tentacles, no teeth; tube feet suckerless. e.g. *Stichopus mollis*.

Other class is the Crinoidea (feather-stars and sea-lilies).

PHYLUM CHAETOGNATHA (arrow worms) and PHYLUM POGONOPHORA (beard worms).

PHYLUM CHORDATA
Body bilaterally symmetrical and with, at least during some stage of development, gill slits, a notochord (a flexible skeletal rod) and a tubular nerve cord (along the back).

Sub-phylum Hemichordata
No tail; distinct proboscis.

Class Enteropneusta, the acorn worms.
Worm-like.
Other class is the Pterobranchiata.

Sub-phylum Urochordata
Tail present only in the larva; adult with an atrium (cavity surrounding the pharynx).

Class Ascidiacea, the sea-squirts.
Adult attached to the substratum, sac-like and protected by a thick tunic. e.g. *Corella eumyota.*
Other classes are the Larvacea and Thaliacea (salps and relatives).

Sub-phylum Cephalochordata, the lancelets.
Adult with a tail and atrium; body segmented.
Sub-phylum Vertebrata, the vertebrates.
Definite head, skeleton (of cartilage or bone) comprising a brain case (protects brain) and backbone of distinct pieces (vertebrae), well-developed eyes; body segmented (shown by muscles and vertebrae).

Super-class Agnatha
No jaws or paired fins.

Class Cyclostomata, the lampreys and hagfishes.

Super-class Gnathostomata
Jaws present.

Class Osteichthyes, the bony fish.
Skeleton bony, gill slits covered by an operculum, over-lapping scales. e.g. *Tripterygium robustum.*

Other classes are the Chondrichthyes (sharks, skates, rays and rabbit fish), Amphibia (newts, salamanders, frogs and toads), Reptilia (turtles, tortoises, the tuatara, crocodiles, alligators, lizards and snakes), Aves (birds) and Mammalia (mammals).

Glossary

Algal   of the Algae (see classification).

Amphipod   a member of the Amphipoda (see classification).

Atrial   of the atrium, a chamber surrounding the pharynx (branchial basket) of a sea-squirt or lancelet through which water for feeding and respiration passes to the outside.

Byssus   the anchoring cable of tough fibres produced by some bivalve shell-fish from a gland behind the foot.

Calcareous   limy, composed of calcium carbonate.

Cerith   a member of the snail family Cerithiidae (Mollusca, Gastropoda – see classification), also called creeper or horn shell.

Cell   the basic structural unit of plants and animals.

Chiton   another common name for the coat-of-mail shells (Mollusca, Amphineura – see classification).

Cilium   (cilia) a microscopic hair-like process of certain animal and plant cells; usually very numerous, cilia sweep to and fro driving particles, fluid or mucus along.

Colonial   of a colony (a group of individuals of the same plant or animal species intimately connected).

Crenate   having even, rounded teeth along the edge.

Diatom(s)   a single celled alga (see classification), cell wall of two distinct halves and impregnated with silica; diatoms are important plants of the plankton (small floating organisms).

Desiccation   the removal of water.

Digitate   having finger-like processes.

Dinoflagellate(s)   a minute free-living alga with two flagella (one running around the body, the other backwards) and, usually, a covering of cellulose plates: dinoflagellates are, like the diatoms, prominent members of the plankton.

Discrete   distinct.

Echinoderm(s)   a member of the Echinodermata (see classification).

Ellipsoidal   like an ellipsoid (egg-shaped, but both ends equal).

Filamentous   thread-like or composed of threads.

Fungal   of the fungi (mushrooms, toadstools, molds etc.).

Hydroid(s)   a member of the Hydroida (Coelenterata – see classification), the sea-firs.

132

Introvert   the anterior part of the body which can be drawn inwards.

Isopod(s)   a member of the Isopoda (see classification).

Microflagellate(s)   a minute, free-living, single celled alga which propels itself along by waving a flagellum (a long whip-like process, like a cilium but larger); these minute plants are members of the plankton.

Moribund   at the point of death.

Nacre   the pearly layer of a mollusc's shell.

Nematocyst   a thread-capsule formed in the skin of members of the Coelenterata (see classification), consisting of a capsule and a fine tube which, when triggered, is turned inside out (the thread, depending on the sort of nematocyst, sticks to, wraps around or injects a poison into any animal which brushes against the thread-capsules); the nematocysts are used for defence and for catching prey.

Nerite   the common name of members of the snail family Neritidae (Mollusca, Gastropoda – see classification).

Nesting   living in a nest.

Nodal point   a point about which the water surface tilts.

Operculum   a lid closing the opening of a snail's shell, a bristle worm's tube or the zooecium (box-shaped 'house') of a sea-mat.

Papilla(e)   a small, bluntly conical projection (the human tongue is covered with papillae).

Papillate   having papillae.

Person   a polyp or zooid, an individual of a colony.

Pharyngeal   of the pharynx (an anterior part of the gut, usually muscular).

Photosynthesis   the process by which a plant makes carbohydrate from water and carbon dioxide using the energy of sunlight.

Polyzoan   a member of the Polyzoa (see classification).

Population density e.g. 20/m²   the number of animals present on or in a square metre of shore (used in this book to emphasize the abundance of particular species).

Predacious   preying on other animals.

Proboscis   a trunk-like process of the head, usually used in feeding.

Pustulate   having pustules (little blister-like prominences).

Sessile   attached to the substratum, but without a stalk.

Siliceous   made of silica (silicon dioxide).

Spicule   a minute skeletal element, often with points, of silica or calcium carbonate, embedded in the bodies of sponges and soft corals.

133

Spire   the whorls of a snail's shell above the aperture.

Sporeling(s)   a very young seaweed (strictly speaking it is the plant which develops from a spore).

Stipe   the stem-like part of a seaweed.

Stopper   a common name for the operculum.

Tellin   the common name (from the Greek telline, a kind of shellfish) for a bivalve shellfish belonging to the family Tellinidae (Mollusca, Lamellibranchia – see classification).

Test   the hardened outer covering of sea-squirt or the shell of calcareous plates of a sea-urchin.

Tract(s)   a region or area.

Tubercle(s)   knob-like projections.

Tunic   another name for a sea-squirt's test.

Umbilicus   a navel-like depression at the base of some spirally coiled snail shells.

Veil   a shelf-like forward extension of the head in some sea-slugs.

Veliger   small, free-swimming larval stage of marine snails and bivalves, recognized by the large ciliated head-lobes, the velum (swimming organ).

Index

Numerals in **bold type** refer to illustrations. Those in colour are given the page reference nearest to the plate.

136

140

NATURAL HISTORY BOOKS FROM COLLINS

A FIELD GUIDE TO THE BIRDS OF NEW ZEALAND
Falla, Sibson and Turbott

"Makes it possible for everyone, amateur and expert, young and old, quickly to identify birds of the wild, and to learn more about them . . . Hearty congratulations to the authors and to the publishers." *New Zealand Herald*

Over 200 birds illustrated   Second Edition — revised

THE NEW ZEALAND SEA SHORE
John Morton and Michael Miller

"A true ecological guide to the long and splendid New Zealand coastline. Illustrated with impeccable clarity and style." *New Zealand Herald*

Over 1,000 animals and plants illustrated. 638 pages.

THE TUATARA, LIZARDS AND FROGS OF NEW ZEALAND
Richard Sharell

"A beautiful book that should be in every nature lover's library . . . well written, beautifully produced." *Hawkes Bay Herald Tribune*

52 colour and 18 monochrome illustrations. 10" x 7½".

SMALL BIRDS OF THE NEW ZEALAND BUSH
Elaine Power

A superbly illustrated natural history book with a two-fold purpose; to delight the eye, and to inform. Most of the birds are life-size or larger, with two or more individuals painted in colour. Text is brief, and devoted to salient information. Size 10" x 7½".

WADERS IN NEW ZEALAND
Elaine Power

"As well as her beautifully executed drawings (both colour and black and white) the artist has provided short descriptions of the birds, where they breed and what they eat . . . an important addition to the New Zealand nature library. It is a beautiful book to have and to treasure." *New Zealand Herald*

BUTTERFLIES OF NEW ZEALAND
W. B. R. Laidlaw

"A beautifully produced little book which provides the answers for New Zealanders of all ages. The colour plates are a delight, the text full of interest and some humour." *Auckland Star*

Size 10" x 7½"

BIRDS OF FIJI IN COLOUR
W. J. Belcher

Twenty-five paintings, sensitively handled and accurate in detail, of Fiji's more interesting and beautiful birds. Very informative text by R. B. Sibson.

NEW ZEALAND INSECTS AND THEIR STORY
Richard Sharell

"One of the most fascinating natural history books ever published in New Zealand" *Christchurch Star*. "Ideally, every school and every home should have a copy of this book." *Otago Daily Times*

200 colour photographs plus many drawings and black and white photographs. 10" x 7½".

NEW ZEALAND SPIDERS An Introduction
R. R. Forster and L. M. Forster

Here are the main facts about the spiders of New Zealand. Written in an intelligible and entertaining way, this book will open many eyes to the truly astonishing lives and habits of some of man's most useful friends. Superbly illustrated with black and white drawings and photographs, and 130 colour photographs. Size 10" x 7½".